IAN SIEGEL
CEO, ZIPRECRUITER

GET HIRED NOW!

HOW TO **ACCELERATE** YOUR **JOB SEARCH**, **STAND OUT**, AND **LAND YOUR NEXT** GREAT OPPORTUNITY

WILEY

This book is dedicated to everyone who is looking for work.

Contents

NOTE: Testimonials used throughout these chapters are retellings of stories gathered over the course of research for this book. They are included for illustrative purposes only and are not intended to reflect the exact words of any individual.

Introduction: Nobody Teaches You How to Be a Job Seeker

"Every part of how we operate has changed because of the internet and mostly for the better. One thing that hasn't improved is the quality of our job candidates. People apply to our jobs with typos in their resumes, come dressed inappropriately for interviews, and what's amazing to me, don't know anything about our business when they get here. I mean why did you even apply to this job!? It's enough to make me want to hire a recruiter. Someone should teach a class on how to get a job. Society has failed these people."

—Frustrated employer

Hi there. Let's have a serious talk. As a cofounder of ZipRecruiter, I have helped millions of people find jobs. But here's the truth. Most of you (I will generously put this at 95%) are terrible at searching for work.

It's not your fault. Nobody trained you to search for a job. Even worse, much of the conventional wisdom about the process has been flat-out wrong since job search went online. But there is good news. I can make you a modern-day job-seeking expert. It won't take weeks of training, or hours of homework and practice. We can do this in a day. I'm not just talking about finding the right jobs to apply to—I mean I can teach you how to write a resume that works, how to stand out when you apply, how to be awesome in every interview you get, and even how to negotiate your job offer to help you get paid fairly.

It doesn't matter what your situation is—I don't care if you are a recent graduate, coming out of the military, coming back into the workforce after a break, or have 15+ years of experience. The advice I am going to give you works for everybody. I am going to give you step-by-step, and *specific*, practical instructions for how to get the job you want and, better yet, how to do it with confidence.

By the end of this book, you're going to enjoy searching for work. I'm delighted to be on this journey with you.

No One Should *Have to Be* Good at This

It's an amazing time to be alive, with technology advancing at blistering speeds. We can talk to our phones, own a car that drives itself, and get medicine tailored to our unique genetics. Drones, 3D printers, electric cars, 5G, artificial intelligence, and smart homes are now commonplace, everyday realities.

All that is happening, and yet the 50,000 job sites operating in the United States today work basically the same way they did when job search first went online in 1999. Even Google, for all its engineering prowess, produced a job site that follows the traditional design—you are presented with a search box and asked to enter keywords in order to find work. When given this self-service search challenge, job seekers struggle to find the jobs for which they are well-suited. No wonder employers frequently complain about lack of "quality candidates" as their number-one issue in business surveys and Federal Reserve reports.

All of us are fundamentally bad at finding the right jobs. But hey—it's clearly not your fault. Does anyone train you to write boolean expressions to get better results out of a search engine? No. Do you even know what a boolean expression is? Probably not.

Why can Instagram and YouTube learn enough about us to serve content we find irresistible, but job search engines operate like choose-your-own-adventure books? Why is job search still so dumb?

The ZipRecruiter "Gulp" Moment

Let me tell you a story...

Before cofounding ZipRecruiter, I worked for a string of early-stage start-up companies that were too small to have HR teams that could do my recruiting for me. As a result I was the one personally posting jobs to multiple job boards like Monster, CareerBuilder, Dice, Craigslist, Hotjobs . . . the list went on and on. (Yes, I am old.) As candidates applied I would have to print out their resumes in order to review them all at once.

The amount of time (and paper) it took was stunning. If I had just three open positions to fill, no matter what my title was at the time, I was transformed into a full-time recruiter. In fact, it was while staring at multiple stacks of printed resumes on my desk, that the idea for ZipRecruiter first came into my head. What if there was a button you could push that would send a job to *every* job site at once? Even better, what if all the candidates who applied were stored digitally in one place for review?

Two years later, that's exactly what my three cofounders and I built. ZipRecruiter was born. We deployed a solution that has not only simplified the recruiting process, but reduced the time to hire for businesses across the country.

When we launched the business in 2010, I was incredibly proud of ZipRecruiter. Employers were getting better outcomes and signing up in droves. The company was winning awards for innovation, and I felt like we'd made a meaningful impact on the world. Hiring, which no one enjoyed doing, had suddenly become easier.

But a couple of years in, something that had been percolating below the surface became too big a problem to ignore. As much as we had transformed the recruiting process for hiring managers, the job seekers we spoke to still *hated* searching for work.

Job seekers didn't know which job sites to search on, which jobs to apply to, and worst of all, why they would send out countless applications and hear nothing back.

The idea of building a better job search experience was daunting. The more we researched, the more we saw it wasn't one thing that was broken—it was the whole process. I remember thinking "this will take years and a *crazy* amount of money to fix." I don't think there was a bigger "gulp" moment in our company history.

Eight years later, with over $200,000,000 invested (yeah, you read that right), hundreds of dedicated full-time engineers working on the problem, and a series of first-of-their-kind features deployed, I am proud to say that ZipRecruiter is the number-one-rated job search app on both iOs and Android. Along the way we had to become experts not just on the technology, but the *psychology* of job search.

Building a better job site meant finding solutions for nonintuitive realities around things like: how job seekers self-disqualify from jobs they should apply to, what recruiters *really* do with your resume, and how speed in everything—applying to a job, responding to an employer's email, or answering your phone can matter as much to you getting hired as your professional experience.

Of course technology plays a big role. The reason Instagram and YouTube can keep you entertained for hours isn't because they have the best content. It's because they have enough data to know what "other people like you" enjoy seeing. This is "the wisdom of the crowd" and it is crazy powerful. ZipRecruiter deployed the same approach to bring you better job matches, and, lucky for us, it works. Software that "learns" is our new reality, and it is getting smarter every day.

But rest assured you won't need a computer science degree to read this book. What you're going to get is straightforward instructions for every part of your job search. You can read the science behind it to understand the "why" (it's all in there), but the important thing is to follow the prescribed advice.

If you were recently **laid off or fired,** are **in school,** are **in the military,** or are **returning to the workforce after a gap in your work history,** I have a list of things for you to do that are time sensitive.

Flip to the back and review the Appendix: "Before You Start the Search."

That's it. No more setup. Let's talk about how to get you a better job.

Get Prepared Now!

1 Accept the Truth About Bias

> *"We give everyone the same interview. It's a standard set of questions to make the evaluation process fair. Interviewers log their evaluations into our HCM [Human Capital Management] system before we discuss as a group who we want to hire. We always objectively pick the best candidate. It just happens to be that most of those people have been white men. It wasn't by design."*
>
> *—White male hiring manager*

I'm going to give you a truth that is difficult to accept. Ready?

No matter how old you are, the color of your skin, what gender you identify with, where you were born, where your family came from, or how much education you've received, you are racist, sexist, ageist, and elitist. You ascribe negative personality traits to people who are overweight. You distrust people who practice a different faith than you. You see people with prominent foreheads as more aggressive. You perceive people with close-set eyes as unhappy. You think people over six-foot-two exude leadership qualities. You categorize people by the clothes they wear, the tattoos they expose, their hairstyles, and even their eyebrows. If someone has symmetrical features, you're mesmerized! You will infer multiple positive character traits about them before they have spoken a word to you. All of that is true about you, and it is also true for every person you meet during the hiring process.

It's not your fault. You're not a bad person and neither are they. Study after study shows *all* humans make rapid instinctive judgments (measured in milliseconds to seconds[2]) and those conclusions are highly unlikely to change with more information.

Bias definitely exists, 100% of the time, and for every job, no matter what the level, no matter what the job category, and no matter what the company. In fact, there is so much bias in the hiring process that combating it with bias awareness training is impossible.[3] Even if somehow I were able to train employers out of all their bias around age, gender, weight, apparel, race, religion, sexuality, and physical features, they would *still* bring bias to the candidate evaluation. And you would too! Don't believe me? Let's play the You Only Get to Know One Thing game!

Pick which candidate is more appealing to you in each of the following scenarios. You only get to know one thing:

1. Someone who graduated from Stanford versus someone who graduated from community college.
2. Someone who worked at Google versus someone who worked at Yahoo!.
3. Someone referred by an existing employee versus someone who came from a job board.
4. Someone who lives in a house they own versus someone who lives with their parents.
5. Someone who uses a Mac versus someone who uses a PC.
6. Someone with a Gmail address versus someone with an AOL address.

None of these "one things" is evidence of the skills required to do the job, yet you infer characteristics about the candidates based on the institutions they've been affiliated with, the brands they prefer, or your initial read of their circumstances. Maybe the person who went to Stanford took seven years to graduate? Maybe the person who worked at Google was fired in less than a year? Maybe the person who lives at home cares for an ailing parent?

Bias exists in all of us. You're going to be judged in seconds on a wide variety of characteristics that seem arbitrary. Guaranteed. So what do you do with this information? You use it! Understanding that bias is everywhere means adapting your approach to turn their bias into your advantage. Job seekers who embrace the reality of bias will give themselves an edge in every stage of searching for work.

Job Search and Bias Are Inextricably Linked

Throughout the next few chapters I am going to explain *exactly* how to make a great first impression at every step of the process. I'm going to tell you what to wear and what to say. Get ready to hack some brains. We're going to make bias work *for* you rather than *against* you.

2 Write a Resume That Works

The rules for writing a resume that works have radically changed over the past 10 years. Not only is the conventional wisdom wrong, following it in many cases will mean your resume is never seen at all. In the next few chapters I'll break down for you how to write a resume that gets into the recruiter's inbox and stands out. None of this is complicated; in fact, writing a resume is easier now than it has ever been. Just follow the advice below.

Write a Resume That Gets Past the Robots

In the modern world, over 75% of resumes are read by a robot before they are read by a human.[1] It starts at the job sites you use to search for work. Every major job site parses your resume to figure out what jobs to recommend. But that's only the first robot that will try to read your resume.

When the majority of job searches went online, the barrier to applying for jobs went way down. This had the predictable consequence of causing a spike in unqualified applicants. To combat this, employers have turned to software. Today, employers (and particularly larger employers) use programs called Applicant Tracking Systems to receive online applications, score them, and rank them. The *sole* purpose of your resume is to get past these robots and in front of a human.

GET YOUR RESUME PAST THE ROBOTS

Here are the most important things to know in order to write a resume that works.

Use the Simplest Resume Template You Can Find

For decades, the conventional wisdom has been that resume design is the first way you can stand out in a job search. When a human was reading through a stack of printed resumes, a beautiful design was a great way to catch their eye. But as I just told you, humans aren't the first ones to read your resume anymore. It's the robots, and *all* of those robots are imperfect. Robots read from top to bottom and from left to right. So your resume should, too. They can only recognize fonts they've seen before. So don't get too fancy. Resumes come in so many different document formats, fonts, and layouts, it's impossible for any of these robots to interpret them correctly 100% of the time. So here's my advice: Guarantee the robots read your resume correctly by using the *most boring* resume template you can find.

I want your resume to look like this:

JOHN DOE

123 Main Street
San Francisco, CA 12345
(555) 234-5678
jdoe@gmail.com

Experienced and capable Forensic Accountant excellent at managing multiple projects and meeting deadlines consistently. Knowledge of various accounting software and processes. Seeking a challenging role where I can continue to enhance client relationships; plans and promote various business opportunities.

PROFESSIONAL EXPERIENCE

ANEERO, INC., Boston, MA
Sr. Forensic Accountant, 2015-2017

- Reviewed analysis of client needs while developing projects to outline the recommended accounting approach.
- Conducted client teams to review results.
- Held monthly seminars for training and development in the Forensic Accounting role.
- Accelerated development of newly hired accounts payable coordinators.
- Redesigned division's monthly newsletter.

SUN LIVE CO, Boston, MA
Forensic Accountant, 2013-2015

- Led fraud and forensic investigations in proper compliance.
- Collaborate with management to enhance expectations of service.
- Supervise developing learning recruiting.
- Delegate work effectively; contribute to performance feedback/training and conduct performance reviews.
- Led fraud and forensic investigation team as well as witness services analyses.

EDUCATION

UCLA, Los Angeles, CA
Bachelor of Science in Business, May 2011
- Honors: cum laude (GPA: 3.8/4.0)

ADDITIONAL SKILLS

- Expert in Microsoft Office, with a focus on Excel
- Trilingual in Spanish, English and French
- Quickbooks, Oracle Financial Training
- Adept at compliance training and systems development

Not this:

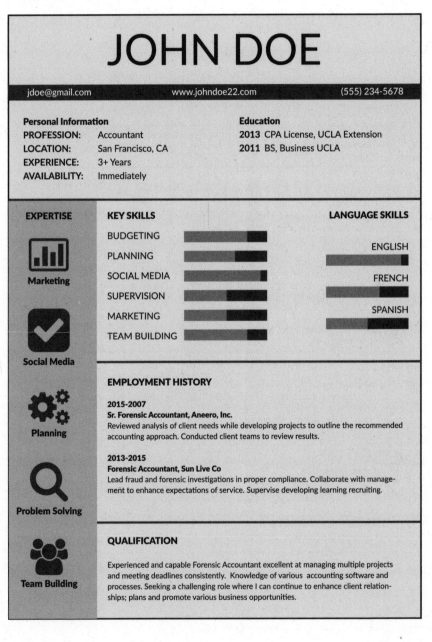

JOHN DOE

| jdoe@gmail.com | www.johndoe22.com | (555) 234-5678 |

Personal Information

PROFESSION:	Accountant
LOCATION:	San Francisco, CA
EXPERIENCE:	3+ Years
AVAILABILITY:	Immediately

Education

2013 CPA License, UCLA Extension
2011 BS, Business UCLA

EXPERTISE

Marketing

Social Media

Planning

Problem Solving

Team Building

KEY SKILLS

BUDGETING

PLANNING

SOCIAL MEDIA

SUPERVISION

MARKETING

TEAM BUILDING

LANGUAGE SKILLS

ENGLISH

FRENCH

SPANISH

EMPLOYMENT HISTORY

2015-2007
Sr. Forensic Accountant, Aneero, Inc.
Reviewed analysis of client needs while developing projects to outline the recommended accounting approach. Conducted client teams to review results.

2013-2015
Forensic Accountant, Sun Live Co
Lead fraud and forensic investigations in proper compliance. Collaborate with management to enhance expectations of service. Supervise developing learning recruiting.

QUALIFICATION

Experienced and capable Forensic Accountant excellent at managing multiple projects and meeting deadlines consistently. Knowledge of various accounting software and processes. Seeking a challenging role where I can continue to enhance client relationships; plans and promote various business opportunities.

If you find a resume template with a name like Minimalist ATS-Friendly, that's the one you want. Be sure to avoid the following:

- Columns
- Tables
- Headers and footers
- Text boxes and sidebars
- Logos
- Nonstandard fonts

Does that mean your resume will look boring? Yes, it does! You *do* have some flexibility. You can use bold, italic, or underlined text, different text sizes, and bullets without tripping up the bots.

Visit the website www.ziprecruiter.com/gethirednow to see resume templates that the robots should parse correctly.

Use Generic Job Titles

Did the last company you worked for call you a "Software Ninja"? Maybe a "Sandwich Artist"? "Customer Guru"? Or maybe they have some sort of clever internal language title like "Project Support Lead—Business Software Systems Level 1."

What do all these have in common? They won't match the job title that any employer currently recruiting will put in a job posting. Remember this: Robots *love* a perfect match. When you write your resume, I want you to change whatever fanciful or confusing job title your last employer gave you to the most generic, commonly used description of the job you did. Wondering what that is? Go to a job site and try to find job descriptions that match your previous role. Whatever title the employers are using to advertise the opportunity, *that's* the one I want you to put on your resume.

But be careful here! If you do change your actual job title to a generic job title, make sure you don't inflate your title inadvertently. If your official title is currently "Director of Customer Happiness" and you change it to "Vice President, Customer Satisfaction," employers may view it as intentionally misleading unless you have a good reason to do so.

> *"I jokingly gave myself the title 'senior relocation specialist.'*
> *I am a pizza delivery driver."*
>
> —*Senior relocation specialist*

Write Like a Caveman

One of the classic pieces of conventional wisdom you'll hear about writing a resume is to "dress up your accomplishments." Some people will tell you to inflate the importance of whatever responsibilities you had, imbue a little grandiosity into your otherwise pedestrian tasks. In the old way of writing a resume, you didn't just "answer the phones" at your front desk position, you "oversaw company communications"!

Well, the robots have changed the game. Not only are they sifting through your resume to understand who you are, but they are also pulling snippets to present a summary of your background to a human. The humans will often read that summary to decide whether to even open your actual resume! You want to make *sure* everything you write is not only easy for

Write like a caveman

the robot to understand, but also explains your capabilities as succinctly as possible for the summary.

Here is an example of how to write like a caveman. This is not the time for prose:

Good:

- Managed a team of 25 for 3 years.
- Built workforce capacity plan.
- Was in charge of all hiring, scheduling, and terminations.
- Improved margins 10% by reducing employee turnover.

Bad:

- Pursued the single most important initiative in the company, which was staffing up for the seasonal surge over six months. Utilized multiple recruiting methods including job boards, social media, and recruiters. Successfully increased team size by 100% under budget and on time.
- Managed every aspect of the team's operation from modeling how many people we would need, to who got hired, to the shifts people worked, to performance reviews.
- Through operational improvements and reduced turnover was able to improve company margins by 10% and received internal recognition from the CEO for most significant contribution of the year.

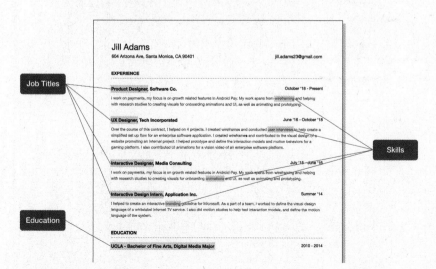

FIGURE 2.5 Robots extract information from your resume.

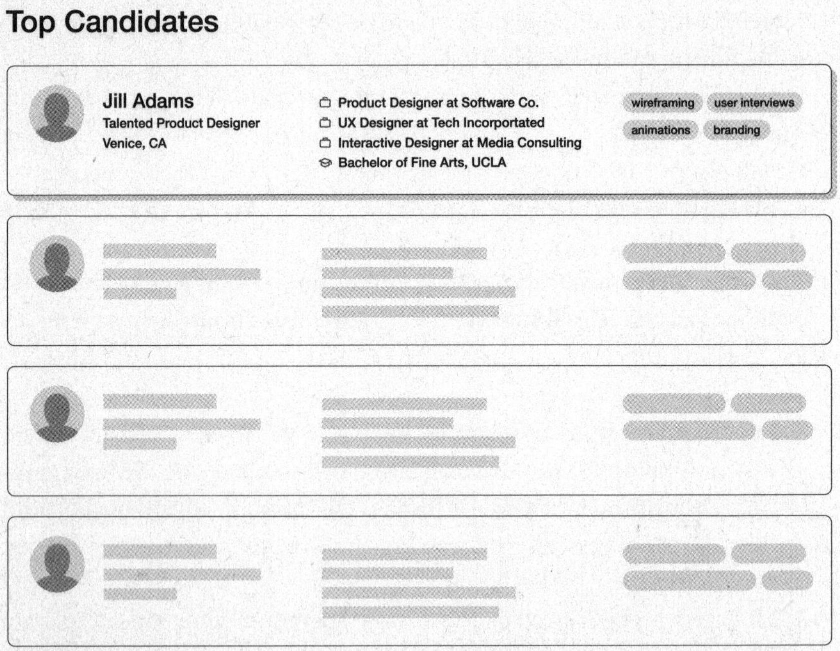

Top Candidates

FIGURE 2.6 Extracted information is presented to employers as a simple summary.

I know the idea of writing like a caveman makes some of you uncomfortable. You think it undersells who you are. Well, remember this: According to multiple studies, recruiters look at a resume for as little as 7.4 seconds.[2] The only thing they are scanning for is whether you have the qualifications to do the job. Make it easy for both the robots *and* the humans to read. Write like a caveman.

Use Numbers to Describe Your Impact

One of the things a lot of job seekers miss is describing not just what they did, but the results of their work. Many people think listing tasks is enough. Take a look at these two examples and tell me which candidate seems more interesting?

Candidate 1:

- Wrote press releases
- Managed PR firm
- Ran the company customer conference

Candidate 2:

- Wrote 18 press releases over 12 months
- Managed $3M annual PR budget and strategy including management of outside firms
- Ran the company customer conference with more than 8,000 attendees over two days

See the power of numbers? *Always* talk about your impact in numbers. I don't care what your last job was. "Made over 1,000 burritos per week to order" is better than "burrito maker."

One Million Anything

My number-one pro tip for talking about your accomplishments is this: one million anything!

There are many ways to use "one million." Few things jump off the page in quite the same way.

- One million visitors
- One million orders
- One million dollars
- One million recipients
- One million customers
- One million people

Nothing screams "this person has experience" like dropping the "million bomb" into your resume. Maybe it's the size of the budget you managed? Or maybe it was the number of people in attendance over a season that you worked security at a stadium? Or maybe it was the circulation of the magazine you wrote content for? However you get it in there, get it in there. "One million" has the ability to make any work experience intriguing.

List Job Skills and Be Explicit

"I swear, if I see one more person applying for my graphic design position and listing out 'Adobe Photoshop' as one of

> *their job skills, I'm going to scream! If you're interviewing for a graphic design position, I'm going to automatically assume you're familiar with Photoshop, because if you're not, you have no business applying! Don't just tell me that you have the skill, tell me what you can actually do with that skill!"*
>
> *—Employer who needs more information*

In a traditional resume, your job skills are typically the very last section. But that doesn't mean it's not an important section.

The first skills you list should be those that are most relevant to the job you are seeking. And when describing your job skills, it's important to describe them as *explicitly* as possible.

Weak:
- Accounting skills
- Familiar with Microsoft Excel
- Microsoft Windows support

Strong:
- Double-entry cost accounting—7 years
- Microsoft Excel revenue model building—3 years
- Certified Microsoft Windows administrator—5 years

More and more, employer job postings are prioritizing specific, demonstrable skills, which is why listing your skills and years of experience benefits you. The robots and the hiring managers are looking for that one primary skill requirement before moving you along to the next step in the hiring process.

After you've included job skills that are relevant, you can include a few "less relevant," non-job-related skills, but only if they're exceptionally unique or interesting. Examples of some good, non-job-related skills to list are: "Certified chess master," "New York City swing dancing competition runner-up," or "Minor league baseball player for the Charlotte Knights—2 years."

You might not think skills like these make sense to include in your resume, but an employer might see those skills differently: a chess player can demonstrate an ability to think strategically, a dancer understands the importance of small details, and athletes know how to work on a team. If nothing else, your odd or unusual skills might generate more interest in you as a candidate, and may be good conversation-starters in an interview.

Check Your Resume for Grammar and Spelling

Imagine you're meeting somebody for the first time. They are fit. They are tall. They walk into the room in a tailored suit.

With a confident smile they reach out to shake your hand . . . and they have lettuce stuck between their front teeth. What do you think you're going to be focused on? If you're a member of the human race, the lettuce will be all you see. You won't hear or remember anything they have to say. In your memory, this person will forever just be "the lettuce person."

That is what poor spelling and grammar is on your resume. Lettuce in your teeth. And before you decide that employers are willing to overlook spelling and grammar errors, let me share a truth we learned at ZipRecruiter.

Every time we've asked employers if they would like us to automatically correct spelling and grammar on job seekers' resumes, 100% of them have said "no." Employers consider those errors a signal about a candidate. Errors say: "This person has poor attention to detail. This person is not conscientious or careful. This person does not understand how to present himself or herself professionally."

Double-check the spelling and grammar on your resume, and then have at least one friend review it for spelling and grammar errors. If you actually get your resume in front of a human, it would be a shame not to get an interview because of typos.

> "I once read a resume that stated the person was the 'validvictorian of my class.'"
>
> —Face palming employer

Resume Writing 101

The lowest hurdle you'll face in your entire job search journey is getting the resume details right. And yet, even with an abundance of resume templates and thousands of articles online giving advice, *many* people still screw up small details that make a big difference in their ability to get hired. You don't have to read this entire book to get a job, but if you're prioritizing sections by importance, this one goes near the top. Make sure basic information on your resume isn't the reason you don't get past the interviewer's door.

> *"We narrowed our candidate pool down from over a hundred applicants to a top five. One of those five stood out above the rest, and that was the first person I tried contacting. That's where I ran into problems. When I called the phone number on the resume, not only did no one answer, but I couldn't leave a message because the mailbox was full. The email address provided was their work email from their previous job, and messages sent there returned an auto-reply stating the individual was no longer at the company! At that point I gave up and moved on to the next best applicant on our list."*
>
> —*Perplexed employer*

Let's quickly walk through each section of your resume. This stuff is easy to get right!

Your Contact Information

Full legal name
- Include the name you wish to be called by and indicate the pronunciation if your name is complicated.

Phone number
- Use your cell phone number or the number that you most reliably answer.

Email address
- If you are in college or graduate school, it is a good idea to use your official school email address. It shows employers that you really attend the school you say you do.

- If you are already in the workforce, use your personal email address, NOT your business email address. Your job hunt is none of your current employer's business.
- Your personal email address should be professional. Email addresses like sexy87@gmail.com or boozehound69@gmail.com will immediately land you in the "no" pile if you get in front of a human.
- There is real bias over what email provider you use. Time to drop the @hotmail.com or @earthlink.net email address and upgrade to something like Outlook or Gmail.

Physical address

- Include your city, state, and zip code.
- If you're open to moving or explicitly looking to move, include "open to relocating" or "planning to relocate."

A Resume Summary Statement

- This isn't always necessary, but may be good to include, particularly if your work experience is extensive and/or your resume is longer than a page.

Your Work Experience

This is the most important part of your resume, so put some real thought into highlighting your most impressive accomplishments, responsibilities, and contributions. Employers want to see where you've worked, what you've done, and what impact you've had.

- For each job include your generic job title, company name, and job location (just city and state).
- For each job, include two to four bullet points about what you did. Wherever possible, include not just what you did, but the measurable change you made. ("Found cost savings that improved profit margin by 12%.")
- Organize work experience with most recent first, to least recent at the end.
- If you have a lot of work experience, only include the most recent jobs. Your resume should never be more than two pages.
- Don't forget the extras! If you work in a creative field, include a link to your portfolio or sizzle reel. Extras don't have to be things you do

for a living. If you're an amateur photographer, show off your creative side by giving them a link to your work. Use *anything* you can to help you stand out.

> *"I got booked for a two-hour time slot of interviews, but the first interview ended after 30 minutes. They told me I could go home. I thought I had screwed up for sure, but literally the next day, they called and made me a job offer. It wasn't until a week into working there that I found out what happened: Before my interview, my new boss had visited the link I included on my resume to my YouTube channel and watched many of my videos. (I did a series of how-to home repair projects that had nothing to do with what I was hired for.) She told me she felt like she already knew me, and that I'd be right for the team. It was the first time I got hired for a job almost before I had walked in the door."*
>
> *—Toolbelt-wearing employee*

Your Education

- Only list your high school education if you graduated within the last few years and have not completed any other higher education.
- For colleges and advanced degrees, include the name of your school, the city and state of the school, the degree you received, and any honors you received.

Your Skills

- Include any skills that are relevant to the job. Be precise with the skills description.
- Include number of years of practice with the skill.
- Include any licenses or certifications you've received. For licenses, include your license number. Any third-party validation of your skills is of benefit to list including training courses completed and/or any ongoing training you are engaged in.

Key point: You don't win a job with your resume. You win the chance to be interviewed.

What If You're Coming Out of School with No Prior Work Experience?

Just graduated from school? Congrats! That's an accomplishment in and of itself. The nice thing is that you're not expected to have work experience. If you do, be sure to include it, whether it's an off-campus job, dorm RA, dining hall cashier, or computer lab help desk.

Next, make a list of all your school experiences from academics, jobs, internships, extracurriculars, community service, and any other productive way you've spent your time. Try to find the thing you're proudest of or most passionate about and make it the centerpiece. Just be thoughtful about how you position yourself. (Did you throw an epic all-you-can-drink frat party that awarded pizza coupons for the longest keg stands? *No!* You ran a fraternity fundraiser that raised $500, and sourced prizes from local businesses.)

For recent graduates, include an Education section near the top of your resume since school is the longest "job" you've had. Include your GPA, or GPA in your major if it's significantly higher (but label it as major GPA). If both of those numbers are bad, that's okay. Just leave them off. A secret they don't tell you until you're in the real world: No one will ever ask you about your GPA unless you bring it up first.

Finally, 93% of employers say soft skills play a critical role in their decision about who they want to hire.[3] Those soft skills include things like showing up on time, willingness to learn, enthusiasm, and a can-do attitude. When you don't have work experience to sell, remember that you can still sell yourself.

Be Honest About Gaps in Your Work Experience

Many people have gaps in their work experience—years where there is a conspicuous absence of work. Here's the most important rule about those gaps: be honest about them. And here's the second most important rule about those gaps: build a narrative around the gap for the recruiter so they don't do it for you. Sometimes a well-crafted narrative can make you more attractive to employers, not less. Own the gap. Treat it like any other work experience. Here are some tips for how to turn gap "lemons" into resume lemonade.

If You've Been Laid Off or Fired

Whatever you do, don't pretend you're still working at a company if they've fired you or laid you off. It's much better for a new employer to hear the truth from you than to get the wrong idea and look like a fool when they call your old employer to do a reference check. So do *not* fudge the end date of your employment and state "to present" if that does not apply.

If you were laid off from your most recent job, you can optionally include a bullet saying so below the job title, company, and date of employment. You could say something like "Laid off in company-wide downsizing effort due to Covid-19 pandemic" or "Laid off due to plant closure caused by falling oil prices." An alternative is to put "Laid off due to Covid-19" or "Department eliminated" or "Location permanently closed" in parentheses after the date of employment. You should only do this for your most recent job.

If you don't want to use up real estate on your resume and you plan to submit a cover letter (often unnecessary, but more about that later), you could mention the layoff briefly there instead.

If, on the other hand, you were fired from your last job, it's best not to mention that on your resume. Let your resume get you past the bots and through the door. Then, if the issue comes up during the interview, you can explain your side of the story there.

> *"I had a job for two years managing a restaurant that should have been called Crazy Town, because the owner was nuts. It was a week after I got a butterfly tattoo on my forearm that I was fired. (We had no policies about tattoos so it came as a shock.) The owner gave me a termination letter detailing my 'poor choice' and encouraged me to seek improvement through*

a closer relationship with 'our lord and savior Jesus Christ.' When I was asked about it in job interviews, the only thing I said was 'I learned the importance of picking a job where I was not just qualified, but also a cultural fit.' Obviously I was pushed for the story, at which point I produced the letter and showed them the tattoo. My new boss and I had a good laugh about it together during the first interview."

—Former employee/resident of Crazy Town

Raising Children

Instead of leaving out the five years when you stayed at home to raise your children, list your occupation for 2011 to 2016 as "Stay-at-Home Dad." Make it humorous, or at least engaging. For example:

- Raised three children—ages 7, 4, and 2.
- Changed 6,729 diapers.
- Reduced "crying time" by over 63%.
- Only one emergency room visit, which resulted in absolutely no visible scars.
- Received "best dad" award from subordinates four out of five years.

"Instead of being defensive about being a stay-at-home mom, I decided to use it. I built an online portfolio of my 'work,' including collages of their first days at school, their National Honor Society certificates, their straight-A report cards, their sports team group photos, and a printout of their criminal background checks, which of course were blank. I even had my husband and my kids write me letters of recommendation."

—Employee and mother of good kids

Figuring Out What You Really Wanted to Do

If your resume gap years were spent "figuring out what to do with your-self," don't be afraid to list that. But be specific and focus on the things you did that encouraged growth. Describing a two-year stint in your mom's basement as "Found Myself (May 2012 to October 2013)" might not be the best way to go.

Rather than giving the resume gap a label, list the years themselves as the experience: "2012–2013: Explored career options while completing online certifications." That description says exactly as much as it needs to while also giving a prospective employer a sense that you did something productive with your time, and that you are honest.

Incarcerated

If you've been incarcerated, it is important to include that on your resume. Most background checks will include the time you served and the category of offense. You don't want that to be the first time a prospective employer finds out about your time served.

For the time you spent in prison, simply list the institution, the years you were incarcerated, and be sure to note that you were released early for good behavior if it applies to you. You probably don't want to or need to be specific about exactly what landed you there, but you should list the category of offense to give some context.

You want to show a prospective employer that you used your time on the sidelines as best as you possibly could to improve yourself. Focus on any facts of your time in prison that reflect well on you and your character. List any skills, work, or activities you did there, including any rehab or coun-seling programs you completed. Most important, try to override employers' biases against former prisoners by including a line such as, "Paid my debt to society for a mistake I wish I had never made, and came out a better, more mature, responsible person in the end."

Caring for Someone Sick (Possibly Even Yourself)

About 39.5% of men and women will be diagnosed with cancer at some point during their lifetimes, according to the National Cancer Institute.[4] And cancer isn't even the leading cause of death. So the experience of having to take time off to undergo medical treatment or to care for ailing parents, spouses, children, or other loved ones is much more common than you might think.

The best approach is to be brief and matter-of-fact without providing too much information. Medical privacy is important, so it's best not to list the name of the person who was ill or the specifics of their condition if you were a caregiver. But you could say something like this:

Leave of absence   5/2019–10/2019

Full-time caregiver during family member's illness

If you are applying for jobs in a field like healthcare or social assistance, you could provide more information if it is directly relevant.

If you are the one who was sick or injured, then you could describe your gap in a similar way. Note that the main question employers will have is whether you are able and willing to work now, so you could address that directly. Here are two examples:

Medical leave of absence due to accident   5/2019–10/2019

Fully mobile and cleared to work by physician following surgery and six months of rehabilitative therapy

Medical leave of absence due to illness   5/2019–10/2019

Condition fully managed after 6-month treatment regimen

If your resume has a more conversational or humorous tone, and you're comfortable sharing more specific information, you could do so, although you are certainly not required to. For example, if you spent several years battling cancer, you might want to describe your gap this way:

Beat cancer   10/2017–10/2019

Just note that if you do provide details, you should be prepared to talk about them and turn them into strengths. Perhaps your time as a patient or caregiver increased your grit, gave you a deeper sense of perspective, and made you want to make the most of every moment in your new job.

> *"I thought quitting my job to care for my mom was going to be a strike against me when I went back to work, but I couldn't have been more wrong. Employers understood I sacrificed so*

I could take care of a sick relative. Most employers want that type of person working for them. "

—Employee and Employable Son

Should You Pay for a Resume-Writing Service?

If you're like a lot of people, putting pen to paper and writing absolutely anything is a painful process. Writing a resume is even more painful than usual because it's not just writing but also "selling," which doesn't come naturally to most people. So is it worth the money to hire a resume-writing service to help you write or refine your resume?

Well, let me answer that question by asking you another: Every year, you have to change the oil in your car. Is it worth paying money to somebody who changes oil for a living to avoid doing it yourself?

I'm a big fan of resume-writing services because they spend all day, every day doing for a living what you haven't done for years: writing resumes. They specialize in perfecting a small part of the job search process that is integral to your success.

Now it's true that, if you take all my resume advice, you shouldn't need any help in writing your resume. But for some people the gap between reading about best practices and actually implementing best practices can be a big divide. And so, if you're one of those people, hire a resume-writing service. In fact, even if you're not one of those people, it's probably worth the money to get an extra set of eyes on your resume to see if they can find small improvements that you didn't think of. (This won't necessarily break the bank. Resume writing services can cost about $100 or even less.)

Just make sure you do your homework and use a service that is competent and reputable. It's easy to find reviews. And always make sure that, whatever suggestions they make, you still follow the rules and suggestions I set out for you earlier.

Give Your Resume the Robot Test

Once you've got your resume done, it's time to confirm that a robot can read your resume The easiest way to do this is to upload your resume to ZipRecruiter—as a .docx or .pdf file, *not* as an image. Our ZipRecruiter *robots* will try to parse your resume and turn it into an online profile. By reviewing the profile, you can see whether the information you included was read and interpreted correctly.

ZipRecruiter happens to be one of the *best* sites on the web at reading your resume. So if your online profile generated on ZipRecruiter has problems, then it's highly likely that MANY other job boards, applicant tracking systems, and screening software programs will have problems as well. To fix the problem, try using a different resume template or different software program until this upload process works without a hitch. If you're using a document you created more than ten years ago, it's a safe bet that you'll need to re-create it using modern word processing software. Remember to keep your resume template as simple as you can find!

Summary

- ☐ 75% of resumes are read by robots before they make it to a human.
- ☐ Simplicity is key when it comes to formatting, descriptions, job titles, and skills.
- ☐ Be honest about your experience; even when you aren't "working," you are acquiring skills.
- ☐ Grammar and spelling mistakes kill opportunities; check and double-check the details.

3 Polish Your Online Brand

Now you've got a resume that works! Congratulations. But before you start searching for jobs, I've got one more task for you. There is a *lot* more information about you available online than you realize. Let's do a quick check. Google your name. I'll wait.

All of us have some combination of Facebook, Instagram, Twitter, Tik-Tok, and LinkedIn. What do all of these social sites have in common? They default your information to be publicly viewable! According to a 2018 Career Builder survey,[1] 70% of employers use social networking sites to research applicants and 57% have found content that caused them not to hire someone.

Time to take a hard look at what you might have posted over the last few years and decide if that's the first impression you want to leave with a potential employer. Alternatively it may be time to set your social site content to private so that potential employers can't review your partying habits, political beliefs, religious affiliation, sports team preferences, relationship status, health issues, drinking habits, position on vaccines, or preferred conspiracy theories.

one year ago today i got so drunk on a tuesday night that i was driven home from the club by the police

9:46 AM • Nov 18, 2020 • Twitter for iPhone

They want my guns I'll give them my bullets first #2ndAmendment #comeandtakeit

11:21 AM • Nov 2, 2020 • Twitter for iPhone

hate when customers show up to my job

2:33 PM • Nov 23, 2020 • Twitter for iPhone

How to Clean Up Your Social Media Accounts

Let's walk through how to handle each of your social media outlets. Every industry has unspoken rules of what is considered appropriate and what may be questionable. Cute kitten memes may be on-brand for someone applying to a pet care start-up, but may raise eyebrows around an accounting firm. The easiest way to handle it is to simply set your accounts to private. Employers can't see what they can't find.

All social media platforms make this easy. Think about what social media you've signed up for and posted on. Even if it was over a decade ago, the Internet never forgets.

Here's how to go private on the big ones. For each, you'll want to start on your own profile page. (Note: Directions may vary based on whether you're using a phone, laptop, tablet, or desktop):

- Facebook: Look under Settings & Privacy and click on Privacy, then review the options to adjust who can see your past and future posts.
- Instagram: Choose Privacy, and tap Private Account.
- Twitter: Go to Settings and Privacy, then Privacy and Safety, and select Protect Your Tweets.
- Snapchat: Hit the Settings icon on the top right corner, scroll down to the Who Can ... section, and select My Friends under each option.
- TikTok: Tap the three dots in the top right corner, hit Privacy, then turn on Private Account.

There are some jobs where you're going to want potential companies to see your social accounts. Some even ask for links to them in their standard applications. Maybe the company wants to see if your passions and interests align with their mission, or the role itself could require social media expertise. But here's the thing: If you can't decide what's appropriate for your own brand, a company won't trust you with theirs.

Go through every picture, article, video, and gif you've put out there and decide if it is something that will reflect well on you. It's not an exact science, but a good rule is that if it's not something you'd feel comfortable saying, doing, or wearing in front of an interviewer, you shouldn't take the chance it will end up on their screen. Each piece of content you've posted over the years will give you an option to delete it. You don't have to delete the whole account, just the pieces you want to remove.

And yes, scroll all the way back to the beginning of your social media life. If you think that taking a trip down inappropriate-memory lane is annoying, you're right. But not as annoying as losing out on an opportunity because you forgot about that body shot contest you won on spring break.

One platform you should definitely *not* set to private is LinkedIn. It's how you'll find employers, and how they can find you. But remember, LinkedIn is a professional social media site. Be sure to review your posts, comments, profile details, and even who and what you follow, to make sure it won't raise any eyebrows.

> *"When one of our job candidates emailed to ask if he could shift the interview from Monday to Tuesday, we accommodated him. The interview on Tuesday went great, and the team loved him. As part of our due diligence before sending an offer, we reviewed his social media profiles. And that's when we discovered WHY he had asked to shift the interview from Monday to Tuesday: Sunday night he was at an all-night rave for which photos of him in various states of sobriety were still being posted at 7 a.m. the next morning. We decided not to hire him, but not because he spent the night before an interview partying. We decided not to hire him because he wasn't smart enough to know not to post photos of himself at a party before canceling his interview!"*
>
> —*Employer who knows how to use social media*

Get Your References Ready

A 2019 survey of more than 2,800 senior managers found that one in three candidates were eliminated from consideration after a reference check.[2] Having good references is critical to landing a job. It pays to get your references lined up as part of your job search prep work. Let's walk through how to get references locked in.

Whom to Ask for a Reference

The best references by far are previous employers and previous co-workers. But don't limit yourself. Some other good references include clients or customers, commanding officers in the military, or even teachers or professors, if you've recently graduated from school.

References from your personal life rather than your work life are unorthodox, but can work in rare cases. Good personal references might be a religious leader, a member of a club or team you lead, or another volunteer in a charitable organization to which you give your time.

Confirm They Will Provide a Positive Recommendation

> *"I don't get it. More often than I'd like to admit, I talk to a candidate's reference, and the reference gives a less than glowing review of the person. Once it got so bad that the reference asked me, in a surprised voice, 'That person really used ME as a reference?!' If you can't find three people who are willing to reliably say good things about you, you've got some real problems."*
>
> *—Employer not surprised by anything anymore*

You need to make sure the references you give are going to say positive things about you. There is only one way to do that—by being direct. Promise me you will come right out and ask every potential reference, "Are you able to give me an unqualified, positive recommendation?" If you have any doubt about their conviction, choose a different reference. References can't get you the job on their own, but they can lose the job for you.

Reconnect Every Time You Give Their Information to a New Employer

> *"I once called a reference for a candidate, and the reference couldn't even remember ever working with the person."*
>
> *—Employer who maybe can still be surprised*

Even when you're doing everything right, the job-seeking process can sometimes take months, and as a result, a lot of time can pass between the moment your endorser agrees to help you and the moment you actually need them to be a reference. Don't let them be surprised by a call out of the blue from a prospective employer you're interviewing with. Reconnect every time you want to use them as a reference.

Just before you share their contact information, either text or call to let your reference know the name of the person who will be calling them, the company they work for, what that company does, and most importantly, specifics of the job you're applying to. The more they know about the job and what you'll be tasked to do, the more they can tailor their comments to the particular strengths that make you a standout candidate.

Your reference wants to help you. Make sure you set them up to be successful.

Get Your Recommendation Letters in Place

Write Your Own Recommendation Letter

A recommendation letter is frequently used by people earlier in their career and/or in situations where the reference giver is unable to lend their time to live calls. (Examples include teachers, military superiors, elected officials, or prominent executives to name a few.)

A recommendation letter is a more concise, written version of a reference, but with one big advantage—you can custom-tailor the letter to deliver exactly the message you want by writing it yourself.

Am I suggesting that you write a recommendation letter, sign somebody else's name to it, and submit it to an employer? No. It's never acceptable to forge a recommendation letter. However, what is *quite common* is to write a first draft of the letter for your reviewer, and allow them to edit it as they would like for the final version.

It takes a considerable amount of time and effort to write a good recommendation letter. Some of the people you ask to write a letter will be more likely to help you if you make it easy for them. If you do end up writing a draft of the letter for your recommender, there are four things every letter should have:

A Clear Opening Statement

The opening statement should describe who the reviewer is, paired with a strong endorsement.

> My name is Eric Smith, head of sales at Left Foot Shoes, and I am writing to offer my highest recommendation for Michael Thomas.

> Make sure to use a descriptive adjective up front like *highest* or *full-throated* or *enthusiastic*.

A Description of the Professional Relationship Between You

Make sure to include a precise description of how the recommender knows you and the length of your relationship. For example:

> I directly managed Dwight for three years in his role as Assistant to the Regional Manager.

Concrete Examples of What You Did Well

To maximize the effectiveness of a recommendation letter, it should specifically identify what you did well, and tell at least one story about what makes you stand out.

> Not only was Jen good at the little things like showing up on time, accurately counting out the register, or restocking the shelves, she was also good with people. We had a recurring problem of unchaperoned high school students trying on multiple pairs of shoes and taking pictures, but never making purchases. Rather than bring the issue up with the school or mall security, Jen spoke directly to the kids about the problems they were causing for the store. She was straightforward, and respectful. The kids stopped coming by after their talk. This was just one example of how Jen made an impact beyond the scope of her role.

An Endorsement of Your Future Potential

No recommendation letter is complete without a big compliment at the end. Just remember that if you're drafting multiple letters for recommenders, you'll want to vary the language you provide.

> I have no doubt that David will succeed in any role in the shoe industry—or in sales of any kind. Based on his three years of hard work at our store, I know that he will be an asset to any future employer.

Summary

- ☐ Employers will look at your social media accounts; clean them up or set them to private.
- ☐ Be proactive about job references and don't be shy about giving them the words you'd like them to say.

4

Network to Build Relationships

If you want to go fast, go alone. If you want to go far, go with others.

—African proverb

Networking Is an Awesomely, Ridiculously Unfair Advantage. Use It!

The world isn't fair. Many times even if you have the right skills, you don't get the job and the most common reason is "somebody had an in." Somewhere between 60%[1] and 85%[2] of jobs are filled by networking. It's how the world goes round. People don't make hiring decisions on the best resume and qualifications alone. They put a lot of weight on who you know and who will speak well of you.

The job search, and much of life, is about relationships. Those relationships are built upon a foundation of networking. Unfortunately, a lot of people are as uncomfortable networking as they are with public speaking or asking someone on a date. It raises the specter of rejection without a clear idea of what success looks like.

But like it or not, afraid of it or not, a strong network is often what sets the person who gets hired apart. If you aren't building a network, not only may you lose out to someone less qualified than you today, but you are missing out on opportunities in the future. Many job openings never get posted or announced because the hiring manager creates the role internally to bring a specific known candidate in.

The bias toward "known individuals" is something everyone has. It's tribal and coded into our DNA. Don't think you have this bias? Ask yourself if any of the following sentences are true for you:

- "When I go to a party I talk to my friends and the friends of my friends before I introduce myself to new people."
- "I am more likely to make positive assumptions about somebody when someone I consider competent has respect for them."
- "At work, I would be more inclined to hire someone a current employee vouched for over a candidate from a job board."

In short, the world runs on relationships, and networking needs to be a major part of your job search strategy.

> *"I'm at the stage of my career now where almost every sale I make, every deal I close, every job I get hired for, has been directly as a result of my network. I don't think I've cold-called anybody in over a decade. After 20 years in the business world, I can honestly say that at least 80% of the value I bring to an employer now is due to my network and Rolodex. It's true: It's not what you know, but who you know."*
>
> *—Employee in need of more Rolodex cards*

How to Network

According to research from Columbia University, the average person knows 600 people in total,[3] but only between 10 and 25 well enough to say they trust them. That's a strong foundation, but how do you use that network to help you?

The Strength of Weak Ties

In his doctoral thesis, famed sociologist Mark Granovetter revealed how social networks help us land jobs. The key insight? It is our weak connections, and not our strong ones, that actually make a difference.[4]

The people you do not know well, with whom you do not have a shared history, and who you do not see on a regular basis—*those* are the ones who will help you the most. It makes sense. Who do your good friends or professional connections know that you don't?

Invite Everyone You Know (and Don't Know) to Connect on Social Media

> *"One of the best things I've done over the years is connect with almost everybody I meet through LinkedIn, regardless of whether I meet them through business or my personal life. I've connected with my plumber, some guy I met for ten minutes in line at Starbucks, and even my old teachers from high school. I now have several hundred connections, and no matter what company I'm interested in, I almost always find that I can get a warm introduction from somebody in my network, rather than having to cold-call in."*
>
> *—Employee who just sent you a LinkedIn request*

Now is not the time to be shy. Go to your preferred social network/s, and connect to everyone you can. Don't limit yourself to close friends or past co-workers. All of the following people should be invited to connect.

- Extended family members
- Alumni from your school/s
- Acquaintances
- Second-degree relations (both personal and professional)
- Current employees of companies you previously worked for even if you never met them

- Senior figures in your preferred industry (never hurts to ask)
- Members of clubs or organizations you've joined
- Congregants of your house of prayer
- Members of your military unit

The larger the number of people you're connected to, the more opportunities you create to be a "known individual" or referenceable by a "known individual."

Smash That "Like" Button

Ever wonder what would happen if you "liked" every photo on your Instagram feed? An engineer named Rameet Chawla wrote a script to do just that, which he dubbed "Lovematically."[5] The results . . . he grew his follower count by 30 a day, was invited to more parties, was stopped on the street by people who recognized him, and received repeated requests to post more. He got so popular that Instagram shut him down!

One thing that's clear on social media is you have to "give" if you want to "get." Don't be a lurker. Make your presence felt by actively engaging with the content you see posted. This can be a "like," a retweet, or a comment.

People on Social Media Are Primed to Help You

Sometimes referred to as "the cuddle hormone," oxytocin is a chemical that, when released in our brains, heightens feelings of trust, empathy, and generosity. After spending just ten minutes on social media, a person's oxytocin levels can rise as much as 13%, which is the hormonal spike equivalent of some people on their wedding day.[6]

Understand that you can ask for help on social media . . . and get it. The trick is you can't make asking for help the *first* thing you do. Instead we need you to build up your online brand.

It's Not Just the Subject Matter—Words and Tone Matter

Most of us use social media to dress up or showcase mundane parts of our lives. "Look how great my food looks" or "check out my new apartment" or "see how happy my family is." Psychologists refer to this as "self presentation," which means telling the world how you want to be seen. (You're so good at this visiting your own Facebook profile will boost your self esteem![7]) This is what I call "safe posting." You're doing what everybody does, so it doesn't stand out.

However, if you want your network to help you find work, it's time to think differently. Are you positioning yourself as someone others would want to recommend?

There is an apocryphal story about a person who comes upon three bricklayers working together on a project. He asks the bricklayers, "What are you building?"

The first bricklayer responds, "I am building a wall."

The second bricklayer responds, "I am building a building."

The third opens their arms and looks up at the sky before proudly declaring, "I am building a cathedral!"

Which of these three people would you recommend for the next bricklayer job? All of them were performing the same task, but they had very different descriptions of the work. To network well, you'll need to channel the third bricklayer when you post to social media. Let's get specific.

Share Openly What You're Passionate About

All of us have things we love in life. It's time to tell everyone about yours. A large body of psychological research shows that people are drawn to others who exhibit "perceived similarity."[8] In simple terms, the fastest way to establish meaningful connections is to have a shared passion. Marketers call these affinity groups. But you can just call them "people I find easy to talk to." And passion for just about *anything* will work.

In one experiment,[9] researchers found that people have the same physiological response to photos of product logos as they do to photos of their closest friends and family. The takeaway: If you love your Peloton, go ahead and tell people. Love your electric car? Shout it from the rooftops! Love your Spanish class? Digales todos!

Anyone who "likes" your post is someone worth connecting with. This is a simple tactic for finding PLUs (People Like Us), and this pool of acquaintances might just be the difference in your next job search.

People Are Attracted to Momentum

Does the idea of posting a gym selfie make your skin crawl? Are you embarrassed to share the results of your baking projects? Do you think, "who would care about the class I'm taking?" Well, I need you to put that introversion away. I'm trying to get you a job here, and the investment you make in networking compounds over time. Remember, someone *just being acquainted with you* can be enough to put you over the top when an employer is selecting among final candidates.

When posting to social media, the thing to realize is that while people like baby pictures, they *love* stories. The more you can provide a narrative—progress, milestones, or accomplishments over time—the more interesting you become. Doesn't matter if you're getting fit, upgrading your wardrobe, or rebuilding a car. Before-and-after photos kill. And don't be afraid to take us on the journey with you. You may think it's vain, or bragging, or exhibitionist, but passion is infectious. What you care about becomes interesting to all of us. Talk about some aspect of your life where you have momentum, and share the gritty details. That's how a post (or sequence of posts) gets popular, and your circle widens.

Note, I'm not just talking about Facebook and Instagram. Don't be afraid to let your personal life bleed over into your professional presence on LinkedIn. *Especially* if you're looking for a new job. Are you back in school learning new skills? Tell your professional network. Are you learning a new language? Tell your professional network? Are you playing chess? Tell your professional network. Remember to be vulnerably effusive in sharing your passion. It will expand your network and enchant future potential employers.

One BIG cautionary note. Some things you may be passionate about are so divisive they will reduce your opportunities to expand your network and/or turn members of your existing network into detractors. You'll want to think very carefully before speaking out on any of the following issues:

- Politics
- Religion
- Vaccines
- Conspiracy theories

- Climate change
- Gambling
- Natural remedies
- Guns

In the Real World, Don't Network for a Job, Network for a Relationship

Whether you're at conferences, industry events, or heck, meeting the parents of the other kids at your school, you don't network for a job—you network for relationships. It just so happens that some relationships lead to jobs.

When you meet somebody, especially in a business setting, the most common first question is, "So, what do you do?"

From now on that's the *last* question you ask.

The whole point of networking is to make a personal connection with somebody, and just about the least personal, most utilitarian question you could ask somebody is "What do you do?" Instead, start with the personal stuff. No more small talk. I want you to take them straight to "medium talk"! (Credit to Larry David.)

Aside from getting to know them better, it will also set you apart from all the other people in a room who ask the same unremarkable questions over and over. There's a number of conversation starters out there on the Internet, but here are a few of my favorites:

- What do you do for fun?
- So what's on the top of your bucket list?
- If you could be anywhere right now, where would you be?

"When I was 16, our robotics club in high school invited a Ford Motor Company engineer to speak to our group. Afterward, I sent an email thanking him, and he offered to help if I ever had any questions. Over the years I took him up on that. He wound up advising me on what college to attend, what classes

> to take, what area to specialize in, what graduate school to choose, what thesis topic to investigate, and even what jobs to accept after school. And then, after a 25-year friendship, I applied for and got a job on his team. Who knew that somebody I met when I was 16 would hire me when I was 41."
>
> —Employee and long-term networker

Make the Most of a Formal Networking Meeting

Sometimes we reach out to people in the real world to ask for help or advice. This can be alumni from our alma mater, respected members of our industry, or even just acquaintances.

I encourage you to do this, and to plan ahead so that you get a positive outcome. Here are some quick tips:

- **Be explicit.** Whether it's someone you know or a cold call, be direct in what you're asking for (phone call, coffee, etcetera), and what you'd like to discuss. It's awkward to ask them for a job, but you can say you're looking for jobs in their field.
- **Do your research.** This is not the time to ask questions that can be answered on Google. Look up details about their career and industry so you can demonstrate your sincere interest and be seen as a peer.
- **Align your interests.** People get excited about their own interests. And if your interests align, they get excited about you.[10] Use the research you've done to find common passions.
- **More humble, less brag.** Studies show that people hate hearing humble brags even more than they hate straight-up bragging.[11] You're here to learn from someone who has more knowledge on a topic than you. Impress them with your passion, not your phone contacts.
- **Offer to help.** Just because they are helping you, doesn't mean you can't do something for them. Listen to what they share and see how you can provide value. Maybe suggest a new restaurant or offer to chat with their child applying to your alma mater.

Summary

- [ ] Humans' bias toward "known individuals" makes networking an essential activity.
- [ ] People are biologically predisposed to want to help you, so give them that chance.
- [ ] Social media gives you everything you need to make connections and stay top-of-mind.
- [ ] A job should be the last thing you discuss when you network, but always be ready.

Find the Right Job!

5

Use Job Sites That Have These Features

> *"I'm 64 years old and I don't think this generation fully appreciates how simple finding a job is today. When I got out of school, I searched through classified ads in the newspaper, printed out my resume, wrote a cover letter, mailed all that in an envelope with a stamp I'd have to lick, and then waited three to four weeks for a letter back or a phone call. It makes me laugh when people complain today about how hard it is to find a job."*
> *—Employee who knows things could be worse*

Over the past eight years, job search technology has gone through a revolution, but only a handful of sites have the necessary scale, dollars to invest, and engineering talent to build modern solutions. Let's go through the features you should care about.

Feature 1: Has All the Jobs in One Place

The first disruptive change to the job category happened back in 2008 when the aggregators appeared. Unlike traditional job boards that would only display jobs employers paid to post, aggregators scoured the web to find *all* the jobs from every site, and made them searchable in one place. Aggregators had millions of jobs while old school job boards only had a few hundred thousand. Obviously this greatly expedited job search.

Today there are a handful of sites including ZipRecruiter, LinkedIn, Monster, and Indeed that use the aggregation approach. Each company uses different technology to find the jobs that are out there, so there is some variation in what jobs you'll find on each site. (For example, Indeed excludes the millions of jobs directly posted on ZipRecruiter from their search engine.)

When it comes to job search, any site that doesn't have all the jobs in one place is forcing you to use multiple sites. Who's got time for that!

Feature 2: Enables You to Apply to Jobs with One Click

One of the most frustrating realities of modern job search is that many employers require job boards to send you offsite to the company's corporate job page in order to submit an application. These corporate job pages are not only difficult to navigate on your mobile device, they also often require you to go through a full site registration before you can apply. These experiences are so onerous that very few of the potential applicants who are sent off to a corporate job site from a job board complete an application! No one wants to spend 15 minutes figuring out how to apply to a single job. Fortunately you don't have to.

The best job sites will have done a technical integration with all of the vendors that power these corporate job sites. That means you'll be able to one-click apply to many jobs without ever leaving your primary job site interface. This is a tremendous time saver and makes rejection, should it happen, sting a little less.

If you don't see a "one-click" or "one-tap" apply option on your current job site, or if you find yourself being sent to other sites to apply over and over again, it's time to switch to one of the big modern job boards.

Feature 3: Picks Jobs Just for You

On average, aggregators like ZipRecruiter have north of 6 *million* open jobs at any one time, with millions of new jobs cycling through every month.[1] Searching through all those jobs once can be a daunting challenge, let alone trying to monitor for new opportunities on an ongoing basis. The task is beyond most job seekers. Surprisingly, until recently it was also beyond the capability of all job sites.

One of the most shocking things I discovered about the job board industry back in 2010 when we launched ZipRecruiter is that the majority of job sites were terrible at notifying job seekers about new jobs. Many of them didn't even try to do it. No daily email alerts. No suggested jobs. And the idea of highlighting a single job for which the job seeker was especially qualified—a fantasy. It literally didn't exist.

And then in the early 2010s, everything changed overnight. Technological advances made it possible for companies to build smart software. Everyone calls this "artificial intelligence" (AI).

AI has now been deployed to give you better job recommendations. When AI helps you pick jobs for which you are best suited, employer satisfaction with applicants dramatically improves. On ZipRecruiter, employers give applications a thumbs-up if they want to shortlist them, and a thumbs-down if they want to reject them. When we introduced AI, we saw the thumbs-up rate climb from 15% to 35%[2] over the next three years. These algorithms get smarter the more information you feed them.

Thanks to the emergence of AI, you now live in a golden age where AI can pick "just right" jobs for you as soon as they are posted. ZipRecruiter is at the forefront of this innovation, but others are experimenting with it as well.

Feature 4: Shows You What the Robots See

All job sites use robots to try to extract who you are from your resume. However, most of those sites won't show you the output, and the unfortunate truth is that most of these robots aren't very good at it. The average resume parser is only about 60% accurate in interpreting resumes.[3] To have any hope of getting the right job recommendations, you need to be able to review what the robot extracted, and make corrections if the robot got it wrong.

Look for sites that turn your resume into an online profile that you can edit. Whatever is in the online profile is what the robot extracted. If your resume looks great, but the profile is a mess it's definitely worth taking the time to correct the profile information.

The best sites let you correct, and also enrich the information in your profile. Some will ask you for links to your personal website, awards, license numbers if you're in a field that requires certification, or even additional skills that aren't currently included in the resume you provided. Provide as much information as possible because the modern algorithms are able to use every bit to show you better matches. (And you're helping them get smarter over time!)

> *Key insight: Only use job sites that turn your resume into an online profile you can edit.*

Feature 5: Alerts You to a Job Match *as Soon as* the Job Goes Live

Do you know the absolute 100% best time to apply to a job? *One second* after the recruiter pushes the "post job" button. You want your resume in their virtual inbox before they get up from their desk. You want their mind to still be on the job and curious about who just applied. The best robots are *fast*.

More than 25% of jobs are filled with candidates who applied within the first two days of a posting. Speed matters so much that 50% of hires tend to be people who applied within the first week.[4] The more advanced a job search site's tech, the faster the algorithm can process new postings and notify you if you're a fit. Speed *rules*. Don't waste your time on sites that aren't giving you instant notifications of new job postings. You're giving up a critical advantage.

Feature 6: Enables Feedback on Individual Job Suggestions

Does the job search site you're using enable feedback when it suggests a job to you? Look for the option to give a thumbs up or down on a delivered suggestion or maybe a happy/sad face rating. Sites that have these signals are feeding them back to the algorithm so that future recommendations get better. With this feedback, the algorithm can infer things like salary range, geography, and company size that you prefer so your delight keeps increasing over time.

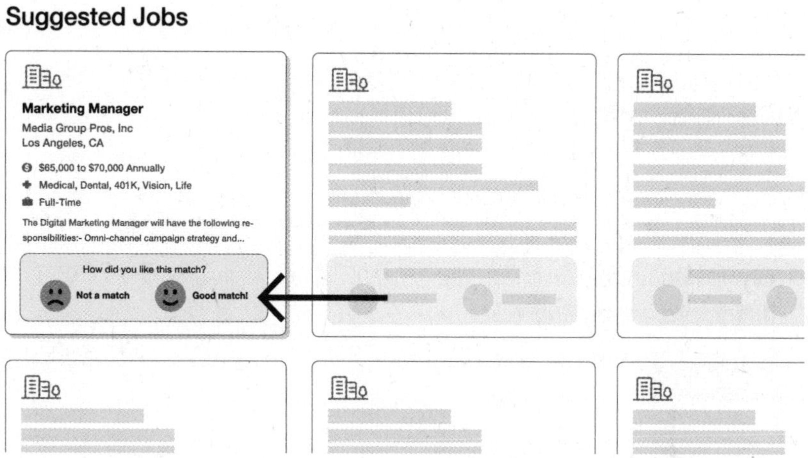

Suggested Jobs

FIGURE 5.1 Use sites that ask you for feedback on the matches they give you.

Feature 7: Shows You How Good a Match You Are for Every Job

The second most common complaint from job seekers after not getting a response to an application is not knowing which jobs to apply to. Job search companies that are *really* using AI now have the processing horsepower to show you how good a match you are for *all* of the millions of open jobs in the country. That means as you browse search results, or review job alert emails, or any other part of the search experience, the site will explicitly call out whether applying makes sense!

Feature 8: Keeps Track of Your Applications

Have you ever applied to a job and been unable to find it again? This happens all the time. When an employer closes a job posting it is no longer discoverable through search. Employers close jobs when they have enough candidates to start interviewing, but haven't yet filled the position.

Make sure to use a service that keeps a record of the jobs you've applied to so you can easily find them again. This is particularly important if the employer contacts you after you've applied. You want to be able to review the details of the position before speaking with them.

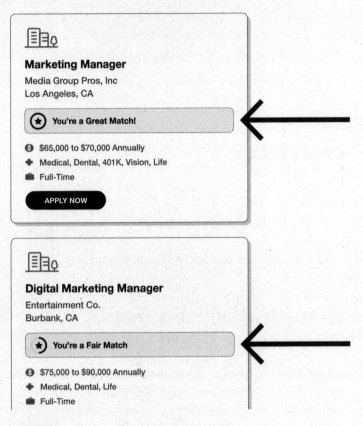

FIGURE 5.2 Use sites that show how good a match you are for every job.

Feature 9: Lets You Know Your Application Status

Here's a funny story for you. Almost a decade ago, when we first interviewed job seekers to figure out what a better job seeker experience looked like at ZipRecruiter, the focus groups would calmly describe the problems they had during the job search process—until they got to what happens after they apply. Then they would explode.

> I apply to jobs, but *never hear anything back*. I don't know if my resume was received. I don't know if I was reviewed and rejected. I don't know if the job is still open. I don't even know if the job was real! I just feel helpless!!

I still remember the focus group moderator telling me, "Yeah. These people are pissed."

Faced with this clear, top priority problem, the team put our heads together to find a solution. It was during this brainstorming session that one of the engineers said "What if I just have the system send applicants emails when the employer is reading their resume?" Good enough, we all agreed. The feature was launched the same day.

And nothing was ever the same again.

Little did we know that our 15-minute discussion, followed by less than one hour of actual software development, would change the trajectory of ZipRecruiter forever. The results were instantaneous and shocking. Job seekers *loved* these messages. Our app review ratings skyrocketed.

From that day forward, our mission at ZipRecruiter has been to give job seekers as much visibility into their applications as possible. Did the employer read your resume? We tell you. Are they looking at it again? We tell you. Did the employer give you a positive rating? We tell you!

There are a few sites now that deliver a similar experience. Once you've had it, you'll never want to go back. This is a game-changing feature for your confidence and optimism during a job search. If you're not getting application status updates, I strongly encourage you to find a site that provides them and see the difference for yourself.

Feature 10: Helps You Get Recruited

Nobody likes applying to jobs, but everybody loves getting recruited.

Sure there is a small contingent of insanely in-demand talent like software engineers or data scientists who complain about "the annoying endless array of recruiters coming after me." But for the rest of us average everyday working stiffs, getting recruited is a *way* better way to discover a new opportunity than actually trying to *find* one. Ask yourself, "What would it be like if the work found me?" Well, get ready. This is the future of job search and the future is already here.

Since "software that learns" has become a reality, the dawn of robot recruiting has begun. What employers *really* want—what they have *always* wanted—is three to five qualified candidates to interview. That's it. The rest of the process—posting a job, receiving 100+ applicants, reviewing the resumes, phone screening, and scheduling interviews—all that is work they *have to do* in order to get to the three to five candidates they talk to in person. Executing all these steps is so time-consuming that employers are literally willing to pay an outside recruiter 25% of a new hire's first year salary to get the recruiter to do it for them. 25%!

When employers post a job the AI presents *you* to the employer! If they like what they see, they'll invite you to apply. That's right—the employers go first. They recruit you! And employers love it when you accept that invitation, giving such candidates a thumbs-up rating almost *70% of the time*.[5] Employers are directly recruiting millions of job seekers per year on ZipRecruiter.[6]

It's fun to think about how this changes job search for you long term. The AI robots make it easy to *always* be prospecting even after you get hired for a new job. You don't lift a finger. Just sit back and let the opportunities flow in. This is the future of job search. You don't apply to jobs. Employers apply to you.

Summary

- ☐ There are powerful technologies that can help you find the right jobs fast; make sure you're using a job site with these features.
- ☐ Feature 1: aggregates all jobs in one place.
- ☐ Feature 2: lets you apply to jobs with one click.
- ☐ Feature 3: shows you personalized lists of job postings that match your skills and location.
- ☐ Feature 4: parses your resume and enables you to edit and update your profile.
- ☐ Feature 5: alerts you as soon as the right jobs are posted.
- ☐ Feature 6: lets you provide feedback on the jobs it shares and learns your preferences.
- ☐ Feature 7: tells you how good a match you are for available job.
- ☐ Feature 8: keeps a record of the jobs to which you have applied so you can refer to them later.
- ☐ Feature 9: lets you know where you stand and updates you on the status of your application.
- ☐ Feature 10: enables employers to recruit you.

6

Tools You *Have* to Use in Your Search

You Must Be on ZipRecruiter

Yes, I know. The cofounder and CEO of ZipRecruiter is telling me I have to use ZipRecruiter. What a corporate shill. Well if I haven't made it abundantly clear already, ZipRecruiter is at the forefront of technological innovation to assist you in your job search.

But hey, don't listen to me. Listen to the wisdom of the crowd. ZipRecruiter is the number-one ranked job search app in the United States for four years running.[1] If you're actively searching for work, and you like the idea of all the jobs in one place, applying to those jobs with one click, seeing status updates when the employer reads your resume, and heck, even getting recruited, then ZipRecruiter is the job search tool for you.

You Must Be on LinkedIn

LinkedIn is *the* professional social network. The number-one way to get a job you want is to know someone who will vouch for you at the company you're applying to. It's also how people in skilled positions or with multiple years of experience are most likely to be discovered by recruiters. Everyone looking for a career versus just finding a job should be on LinkedIn.

LinkedIn gives your network—and the 87% of recruiters who use it to find hires—a *lot* more than your resume can.[2] Used the right way, it can reflect who you are as a professional and as a person. The most important way to do that is by keeping your profile page updated. That means including a profile picture (which increases profile views 21 times and connection requests nine times), listing all of your relevant skills (adding just five skills increases messages 33-fold[3]), your most current experience, and a headline that gives a succinct overview of what you do or aspire to do. If you're looking for work, let recruiters know that you're open to opportunities in your settings. This can be done confidentially so your current employer won't know!

Other information you can use to stand out on your profile includes samples of your work and presentations; listing awards, certifications, volunteer work; and the community and industry organizations you're involved with.

Once you've got your profile in order, it's time to use that search bar!

- Find the pages of companies you are interested in or that fall within your industry and follow them so that their updates and open roles come straight to your newsfeed.
- Look up people you know—current and previous colleagues, friends, and people you'd label "just acquaintances"—and invite them to connect.
- Find people you may not know but have a connection to, such as school alumni, title equivalent peers at partner companies, and even the connections of your connections.

Every person you add to your network extends your circle and gets the messages you share out there. You can expand even further by joining active professional groups on the site. Engaging with other people's content there—and sharing your own—will invite new connections and position you as a domain expert.

You Might Want to Use Industry-Specific Job Boards

The job search industry is replete with niche job boards focused on specific industries. In the majority of cases, the job content on these sites can be found and searched within the aggregators. There are a few exceptions where I'd strongly encourage you to review the niche sites including

Hcareers if you're interested in the hospitality industry, HigherEdJobs if you're a teacher or professional in the Higher Education space, and Rigzone if you're interested in the Oil and Gas industry. If your background and experience are tightly specialized, it never hurts to review industry-specific job sites because they'll often have content beyond just jobs that can either help you network or get more training. I would view these sites as supplements to whichever modern job site you make your primary search tool.

Use a Human Recruiter (If You Can)

The best thing about a recruiter: They're humans who talk to other humans. They can skip the robots and put you directly in front of a real person. Recruiters have connections at many different companies within many different industries, and they know exactly who to talk with to get an interview on the calendar. Sometimes they even know about job openings before they are posted. With a recruiter, you never need to worry about the resume black hole.

Recruiters can also help you fine-tune your resume, coach you on what to say to an interviewer, and are out there on the street job searching for you. The best part is that they make their money from the company who hires you. So all the help they provide comes at no charge.

> *"The biggest value I add as a recruiter to my candidates is that companies trust me to pick the right people for the job, so when I send a candidate over, it's a fast track to an interview. Of course, you first have to convince me that you're right for the job, but if you can do that, you're in really good shape."*
>
> *—Recruiter who can help you*

Monster and Indeed Are Both Good Supplemental Job-Search Tools

The two titans of the old-school job industry are still alive and kicking today. Both of them still do offline advertising, which keeps their brand awareness high, both of them are aggregators that let you search all the jobs in one place, and both of them have enough data to build powerful modern search algorithms.

Monster was bought by Randstad, one of the largest staffing firms in the world. Indeed was bought by Recruit Holdings, a Japanese HR conglomerate also heavily focused on the staffing industry. It remains to be seen how the parent companies of these two sites will use them over time.

One thing we know for sure is that no two sites have exactly the same jobs. It makes sense if you have the time to set up email alerts from one of these two sites as a supplement to ZipRecruiter and LinkedIn.

Summary

- [ ] ZipRecruiter is a must if you're actively looking for work.
- [ ] LinkedIn is a must, but it's a social network more than a job site.
- [ ] Industry-specific job boards work in a narrow number of industries. Using them doesn't hurt, but you should still be on at least one modern general job board as well.
- [ ] Recruiters can give you direct access to opportunities and insight on how to secure them.

7 Apply to These Jobs

You know what sucks? Applying to a job and never hearing anything back. Job seekers around the world call it the black hole. You do *not* want to be black holed.

Here are some guidelines to make sure you get a response and some additional tips for jobs that make sense to apply to.

Apply to Jobs Within the First Two Days They Are Posted

"A job requisition came across my desk on a Monday morning that was a great match for two candidates I was working with at the time. The first candidate told me she was interested and I shared her resume immediately. She had a phone screen that evening, an interview on Wednesday, and by Thursday they were checking references. The other candidate took three days to get back to me. When I sent his resume in, the hiring manager told me, 'He's got great experience, but we're already so far down the road with the first candidate that we don't need more.' The job posting was only four days old. Strike while the iron is hot.'"

—Recruiter who you're really going to want to respond to

Fun fact: 50% of new hires applied within the first week.[1]

In the beginning of a talent search, employers are interested. They want to see what kind of candidates the job posting is bringing in. If you're in that group of early applicants you're also being considered against a much smaller group of competition. The possibility of standing out is greatly increased.

Don't Self-Disqualify

"We intentionally put a lot of requirements into our job listings, but I don't expect candidates will meet them all. Why do we include so many? Well, we either end up with ultra-qualified candidates, we end up with candidates who are so confident learners, which is a positive trait to have."

—Employer who knows you don't fit all the requirements

"But Ian," you say, "I don't fit all the criteria listed under the requirements section for this open job."

Well let me tell you an important truth about job postings. The people writing them are rarely creating a list of actual requirements. What they are creating is a wish list. And often these wish lists bear no resemblance to who actually gets hired.

Talentworks (an organization that studies the science of job search) reviewed nearly 100,000 "entry-level" jobs back in 2018. Of those jobs, 61% asked for one to three years of experience in the requirements.[2] How can a job be both "entry-level" and require multiple years of experience? It can't! Employers are *not* describing who they will actually hire.

From now on when you see the "Requirements" header in a job description, I want you to read that as "Nice to Haves." Give yourself permission to apply for any job where you have 40% or more of what they are asking for.

Apply to Jobs That *Exactly* Match the Most Recent Job Title on Your Resume

The robots that review your application *love* a perfect match. Any time they see that your current (or last) job title matches the job title in the job posting, you have high odds of getting put in front of a human.

And remember what we discussed previously. Many companies use non-standard job titles. Throw that title away! For your resume I want you to use the most common description of the role you filled. No one is reporting you to the resume police for making your work history easier to understand.

Apply to Jobs Where You Know Someone at the Company

This is the holy grail of getting your foot in the door. More than 50% of jobs are filled by a candidate who already knew someone at the company.[3]

When you have someone on the inside vouch for you, they're essentially pulling your resume from the grips of the robots, sidestepping the black holes, and placing you at the top of the list. Not only is it more likely that your resume will be seen by the person with the power to set up an interview, but it's coming from someone the company already trusts. Would you rather hire the babysitter your friend already uses, or take a chance with a total stranger you find on the internet?

Many companies encourage these types of referrals, paying out bonuses to employees that bring in new hires. And there's nothing like a little self-interest to make someone want to help you. It's the job-search hat trick. You get a new job, the employee gets some cash, and the company gets an amazing new hire that's already been vetted.

"We rarely post jobs for our company. Instead, if you want to get hired, you gotta know somebody already on the payroll. If you don't come in with a warm intro, then you probably don't

come in at all. And we trust that, because our employees take pride in our culture and the team we've built. They aren't going to vouch for just anybody to get hired. Personal references are everything, and we far prefer to hire somebody that is a known quantity."

—Employer who is not even going to look at online applications

Apply to Jobs Where You Love the Company, Product, or Service

Companies don't just hire employees. They hire humans—humans with passion. If you're passionate about a company, that enthusiasm will shine through to anyone you meet. Even better, if you love what the company does, there's a good chance you're already an expert on the product, service, or industry they work in. If you can talk about it with enthusiasm— Congrats! You're a great candidate. All companies love a fan who comes in with opinions.

"This candidate walked in the door knowing more about our software than some of us did. She was a power user, an expert, and she was animated when she talked about it. She had ideas for new features we should build and was unafraid to tell us how some current features were letting her down. It was easy to see how somebody like her was going to make us better. Easiest hire we ever made."

—Employer who took the afternoon off after meeting this candidate

Apply to Jobs That Are Closer to Where You Live

Commuting sucks. Whether you're pushed up against a stranger's armpit on the subway, stuck in traffic on the freeway, or fighting freezing winds on a ferry, it sucks. We all have other things we'd rather do with our commuting time.

And besides the cost of gas, parking, insurance, wear-and-tear on your car, plus wear-and-tear on your body—the commute has even further-reaching effects. If you're traveling more than 45 minutes to work, you have a 40% higher chance of getting divorced![4] And commutes don't just kill marriages, they can kill you. Commuters who spend a lot of time getting to work disproportionately suffer pain, stress, obesity, and dissatisfaction.

On the other hand, commuters who have been able to cut an hour off each part of their travel time equated their increase in happiness to that from a $40,000 raise.[5]

The clear message is that long commutes breed misery. And misery breeds unhappy employees who call in sick—or just plain quit. And employers *know* that. Which is why even your proximity to an office engenders bias. It's called the "commute penalty,"[6] and it's real. Employers are going to love it if you live closer to the office and be more weary of considering applicants who live farther away.

Note: 23% of people report having left a job because of the commute.[7]

> *"I pay a LOT of attention to where somebody lives when I'm interviewing. It's easy to say 'I don't mind the long commute' in an interview, but it's another thing when you're living it five days a week. And it's just simple math to say that whatever hours an employee spends on their commute, those are hours that they either can't spend working on the business, or can't spend recharging their batteries with their friends and family. And so I generally won't even interview anybody who lives more than 40 minutes away from the office."*
>
> *—Employer checking your address on Google Maps*

Apply to Jobs with Stated Compensation That Is Higher Than What You Currently Make

About 50% of jobs on ZipRecruiter include salary information in the job posting. The surest way to get a salary bump is to move to a new company. It's a sad fact, since most companies won't give large increases to current employees, yet end up spending more to recruit and train new ones. But that's not the focus of this section. Getting you paid is.

While money isn't a long-term motivator, it is *extremely* motivating in this moment when you're considering new opportunities. The idea of a big payday will drive you to research more, prepare more, and fight for the job more—there's a pot of gold on the other end.

Compensation is a concrete way to compare one job to another and a succinct way to clarify to yourself and hiring managers why you are looking to leave a current role. While there are lots of factors that go into job satisfaction (like avoiding commutes that turn you into a sitting-alone-in-the-dark divorcee), comparing salaries is an easy black-and-white option.

Targeting jobs and companies that offer more money isn't just self-serving. It's an easy way to identify healthy, growing companies. If they are able to offer more compensation, they are likely a stable, long-term place to begin or continue your career.

Lastly, always remember the age-old adage: "Shoot for the moon. Even if you miss, you can land among piles of cash." (That's the quote, right?) The fact that you'd be delighted with their stated salary means even if they don't budge when you negotiate (we'll cover this later, but you *always* negotiate), you'll still be happy with the outcome.

Apply to Jobs at Direct Competitors of Your Current Employer

It's one of the most difficult decisions you'll have to make in your job search because doing this has a high risk of both professional network and personal relationship fallout, but if you want to slam dunk getting a job offer and earn more money fast, try applying for a position at a competitor of your current company. Your industry expertise makes you catnip to the hiring manager as they know you'll hit the ground running, and your inside knowledge of a competitor means you carry a currency that no other candidate on the market can match.

Again, think HARD before you make this choice. Unless you get the blessing of your current company, this strategy is fraught with not just relationship risk, but actual legal peril. Check your employment agreement with a lawyer to make sure you haven't signed a binding noncompete clause. You'll also want to be extremely careful not to bring any of your prior company's intellectual property to your new job—intellectual property has a broad definition under the law. (Don't take a single piece of paper from your old company to your new one!)

> *"I do recruiting for a client whose entire hiring strategy is to target the engineers at a short list of named competitors, and offer 25% salary increases. Their rationale is that these companies have stringent hiring standards, so the vetting process is already done for them. Paying above-market rates avoids the cost of an extended talent search, and incentivizes those new hires to stay longer."*
>
> —Recruiter who stalks other companies all day

Apply to Jobs Where the Employer Has Reviews Online That Pique Your Interest

On average, you'll spend more time with the team you work with than your family. And while you may not be able to read reviews about your family before you join them—you *can* read reviews about a new employer before you apply.

Sites like Glassdoor, Comparably, and Salary.com share feedback from employees on all types of details like work culture, diversity, management, and salaries. Doing this research will give you great content for your interview. And companies love it when you research them! It shows that you're serious about the role and you came prepared.

These review sites are a great complement to your research, but be wary of believing everything you read. Many of these sites show data amassed over "all-time." You could be reading a complaint by someone who left the company years ago. Further, many review sites only have one company page per company. That means a company like Google, with 70 offices in 40 countries has all their reviews combined in one place. Chances are the meeting culture in Melbourne bears no resemblance to the meeting culture in San Francisco. Don't let bad reviews chase you away from opportunities that otherwise look great.

Reading reviews can help you identify the right company for *you*. There are many amazing, world-changing companies that don't have strong employee ratings. Then there are companies that don't have a well-known brand, but people love working there. It's all about personal preference. Having a prestigious company on your business card or resume can pay dividends in terms of salary, title, and offers for the rest of your career. That's very attractive to some job seekers. For others, work-life balance, office culture, and overall satisfaction is more of a priority. These are by no means mutually exclusive, and one is not necessarily better than the other, but reading reviews will give you insight into what might be the best fit for you.

> *"I recently took a job at a competitor to my old employer and accepted a 15% pay cut to do it. Why? My last company paid above-market rates because the culture sucked and that's the only way they could keep people around. The managers were a-holes, politics influenced everything, and HR did nothing about the toxic environment. Now that I'm out, I wish I had left earlier. I forgot what a pleasure it is to work in a professional environment. Knowing what I know now, I would've taken a 30% pay cut to be here. Life's too short not to enjoy going to work every day."*
>
> *—A much happier employee*

Should You Send a Cover Letter With Your Application?

> *"I don't think I've read a cover letter in 10 years. I don't even know how a candidate could submit a cover letter through most of the sites we post our jobs on."*
>
> *—Employer who isn't reading your cover letter*

Much like the sagittal crest in a caveman's skull or wisdom teeth in today's children, cover letters have been phased out by evolution. When job search went online, it transformed the entire application process. There are no more printed resumes mailed to a hiring manager. Now we submit resumes digitally, and it's robots not people who read those submissions. No human opens the envelope, and sadly, in many cases no human ever reviews the application.

These days, I'd say about 99% of the time a cover letter doesn't matter. But what about the other 1%? What about the rare occasion when a human being actually places your resume directly into another human's hands! (Or, more likely, his or her laptop—held by human hands!)

If you find yourself in this incredibly rare edge case, you're a unicorn. Here's an example of how you might gallop your way to success for a Social Media Manager role:

- Address the reader. Find out exactly who the hiring manager is, and use your online stalking skills to find out as much as you can. You want to write something to them directly.

  "Hi Kathy, I saw the Social Media Manager role at [company], which you shared on LinkedIn ..."

- Keep it brief. No one reads anymore. Grab their attention, say what you need to say, and get out.

  "... I'm so excited to apply that I almost tweeted about it! (But then decided it was best to keep my competition in the dark.) The position would be a seamless transition ..."

- Don't rewrite your resume. They already have it. Instead highlight the *main* thing you'll bring to the table. Support that point with numbers if you can.

  "... The position would be a seamless transition from my current role where I increased social engagement by 300%, expanded my client's presence from one social platform to five, and increased social-driven sales by 50% ..."

- Let your personality shine through. Professional doesn't have to mean boring. Especially if the company has a more relaxed attitude. Show that you're a real person, not just a piece of (digital) paper.

"… I've been following your company for years and love the work you do. I even participated in the TikTok campaign you ran. Here's the link. (I promise, I'm much better at social management than dancing.)…"

- Look out for formatting. Do a quick search and base your format off a standard cover letter template. Finish off with a thorough proofread, making sure you look out for things like the difference between to, two, and too.

*"… I'd also love to hear more about the company's commitment to donating one of every **two** dollars it makes to climate initiatives. The environment is something I'm incredibly passionate about, **too** …"*

What If I Want to Change Industries?

According to an annual survey by Gallup, only one in three Americans feel engaged and fulfilled at work.[8] The rest are either "actively disengaged" (meaning they hate what they do) or "not engaged" at all (meaning they put time into their work, but no energy or passion).

You may have a degree or years of experience in a field, but wake up one day to realize this isn't how you want to spend the rest of your life. Or you may be forced to switch careers for another reason. Sometimes an industry is disrupted by a new technology (or maybe a pandemic strikes!) and a whole job category disappears.

However you come to find yourself at a career crossroads, the truth is that the modern job search world can be unkind. The robots don't care about your passion or your hardships. They don't care about what makes you unique and different. There are no "dark horse" candidates in their algorithmic eyes. They are looking for candidates with relevant work experience.

It's a Catch-22: To get a good job in a new industry, you need experience. But to get that experience, you need a job first.

How do you start over and do something new when none of the details of your work history tell the robots you'd make a good candidate?

Be Realistic

The path to a new career isn't always clear. There might be jobs you would love to do and can easily see yourself doing, but the training and experience requirements put them out of reach.

For example, if you suddenly wake up in your fifties and realize you should have become a doctor, that ship may have sailed. Even if a medical school would admit you (and that's highly unlikely), chances are you wouldn't want to go back through years of college courses, medical school, and medical residencies.

But don't despair! There is a rewarding job out there for you and the necessary skills are likely within your reach.

ZipRecruiter regularly crunches the numbers to figure out which occupational licenses give job seekers the biggest bang for their buck, and there are plenty that have relatively minimal training requirements but come with above-average paychecks. These jobs are sometimes referred to as "new-collar jobs"—single-skill jobs that require more education and training than high school, but do not require a degree.

Explore New-Collar Jobs

The economy has become so complex that many jobs are highly specialized. As a result, employers increasingly don't need you to have a four-year degree but *do* want you to have mastered a particular software tool or online platform.

The good news for job seekers and career switchers is that many of the skills in greatest demand among employers can be learned cheaply—or even for free—in a couple of hours on the internet.

High-quality online course providers—such as LinkedIn Learning, edX®, Coursera, Skillshare, SkillSuccess, Udacity, and GoSkills, to name just a few—offer classes and certifications at reasonable prices. And YouTube has millions of video tutorials that walk you through every feature and use case.

In his bestseller *Outliers*, Malcolm Gladwell popularized the idea that it takes 10,000 hours of practice to master a skill. But many software programs are becoming so user-friendly and accessible that they do much of the work for you—no coding necessary.

While it is true that some employers are desperate to hire people who have mastered advanced software engineering, there are many more who need candidates with basic tech skills—the kind that can be mastered in six weeks or less.

Here are some examples of skills and certifications that can give you a big bang for your buck and open the door to well-paid, new-collar jobs.

Drone Pilot Certification

The new capabilities offered by drones are creating tens of thousands of jobs in agriculture, entertainment, oil and gas, construction, insurance, real estate, and delivery. On average, drone pilot jobs get paid $58,000 per year—well above the median annual income in the United States. Drone pilots with photography and video-editing skills can easily earn six figures.

And here's the amazing thing: Although drone pilot programs provide access to a growing number of well-paid opportunities in a wide range of industries, they have *really* low barriers to entry. Earning the "Federal Aviation Administration Certification" typically requires studying for roughly 20 hours to pass a test and a $150 licensing fee. Contrast that with becoming a plumber—most states require you to get 4,000 HOURS of experience and training to make the same salary as a drone pilot!

Photo- and Video-Editing Software Skills

At any one time, there are more than 10,000 jobs on ZipRecruiter for people with photo-editing skills and another 10,000 for people with video-editing skills. Increasingly, these skills are required if you want to be a web designer, graphic designer, photographer, or social media marketing professional, whether in business, entertainment, e-commerce, or tech.

There are dozens of high-quality video tutorials on YouTube—from five-minute beginner tutorials to four-hour crash courses—that can help you build your skills. And there are plenty of image processing courses online, some of which are free of charge.

Even if you don't get a full-time job immediately, you can gain experience and earn competitive pay by putting your skills to use as a freelancer on a freelancing platform like Upwork™ or Fiverr®. There are always people looking for someone to design a book cover or company logo, design an image for a product, or edit a short video.

Sound Production Software Skills

Podcasting has quickly exploded in popularity, with more than 100 million people consuming podcasts regularly, according to Edison Research's 2020 Infinite Dial report.[9] Nielsen projects that number will rise by 20% per year over the next few years.[10]

Rising demand for podcasts means rising demand for people who know how to record a podcast! This includes cleaning up the sound, splicing in effects, queuing up the ads, and publishing episodes to the web. You could become a podcast engineer by investing just a few hours in learning how to record and edit audio using Pro Tools®, Logic Pro, Garage Band, Audacity®, Squadcast, Skype™, Zoom, Ringr, or Zencastr—or any other podcasting tool or service.

Computer-Aided Design (CAD) Software Skills

Another highly marketable skill is the ability to use computer-aided design and drafting software programs, like AutoDesk®, AutoCAD®, or Solidworks®. CAD skills are among the most valuable job skills in ZipRecruiter's Skills Index, which ranks skills in terms of the number of jobs to which they provide access, the rate at which those jobs are growing, the geographic breadth of the job opportunities, and pay levels. They are also relatively easy to learn.

Several YouTube channels offer CAD tutorial videos, from basic to advanced, that are free, quick, engaging, and easy to understand. Spend a weekend watching some videos and practicing some examples, and you could become a competitive candidate for more than 50,000 well-paid positions that are open at any one time on ZipRecruiter at manufacturing, engineering, product design, and interior decorating companies around the country.

Business Management Software

Modern companies use a myriad of software programs to perform their operations. One example is Intuit's QuickBooks® for accounting, accepting business payments, paying bills, and managing payroll. Another is Kronos® human capital management software for human resources functions, payroll, talent management, and timekeeping. Yet another is Oracle's Netsuite® software for accounting, enterprise resource planning, and e-commerce.

Software programs for business management, project management, team collaboration, and office management score highly on ZipRecruiter's Skills Index each year. And many are relatively easy to learn. The software companies themselves offer many training certifications, and you can find playlists of training videos on YouTube.

Other New-Collar Job Skills

Not all new-collar job skills are software-related. There are many other trades that require more training than high school, but less than a college degree. For example, home inspectors take home about $61,000 per year and earning the license only requires 360 hours of training and experience, much of which can be gained free of charge on the job.

Massage therapists typically aren't required by state licensing boards to get nearly as much training and experience as manicurists or pedicurists, but massage therapists earn almost twice as much, on average ($54,639 versus $32,509 according to ZipRecruiter salary estimates).

Licensing requirements for cosmetologists have become so onerous that candidates now need 2700 hours of training and experience, on average, to get paid to cut your hair. That's not much less than the requirement for becoming a Radiologic or MRI Technologist (3,300 hours)—a job that is growing considerably faster than average, is more recession-proof, and pays twice as much ($56,162 versus $28,608, according to ZipRecruiter salary estimates).

Among jobs that require a two-year associate's degree, some pay substantially more than others. The average state licensing fee for becoming a dental hygienist is a hefty $1,600,[11] but the pay bump you'll receive will make up for it ten times over in the first year.

So if you're thinking of finding a new career, do some research and do the math. Important numbers to find include the median salary for a job, your state's occupational licensing requirements (for example, how many hours of training and experience you need to be allowed to work legally, the state licensing fee, and any training course tuition fees). Before you take the plunge, make sure the up-front investment you need to make in developing new skills is one you can reasonably afford, and make sure the payoff is worth it.

Consider Freelancing

Another way to make up for a lack of prior experience when you're switching careers is to freelance. About 59 million Americans freelanced at some point in the past year, according to a survey by Upwork™, an online freelancing platform. That's more than 30% of the United States workforce.[12]

Freelancing can give you schedule flexibility and a way to get your foot in the door. It can also be a way to develop a portfolio of projects and gather references—both of which are extremely valuable when you apply for a permanent job.

Joining a freelancing platform (or more than one) can make it easier to find clients and jobs that you like. Upwork™, Fiverr®, Toptal®, DesignHill, and 99Designs® are just a few examples of online platforms where you can bid on jobs. But know that the internet is a dynamic place, with new platforms coming online all the time. Look into both general platforms and more specialized ones in your particular occupation to explore all the options.

Do *Not* Apply to These Jobs

"I was so excited to get a job so quickly that it didn't even occur to me how strange it was that the interview process was so quick and easy. I filled out the intake paperwork without hesitation, and didn't even get suspicious when they asked for all my bank account information for the direct deposit of my paychecks. It wasn't until they asked for backup bank account information that I began to suspect anything was up, but by then it was too late. They had already wired most of my money out of my bank account. Luckily, I notified the bank early enough that they got the funds back, but it was a painful and time-consuming mistake I made."

—Employee who won't make that mistake again

Watch out for phony employers and job scams. Even though many job search sites use software to detect and remove fraudulent job postings and have entire teams devoted to removing suspicious postings as soon as they're flagged, no system is totally secure.

Many criminals are highly sophisticated and can fool you into thinking they're offering a legitimate job opportunity, even if they're really operating an illegal operation.

There are many scams out there, designed to take advantage of people who are desperate for work. Remember, you aren't desperate! You've got this book to help, and you're on your way to getting hired.

Scams are so common that the Federal Trade Commission is constantly clamping down on them and publishing warnings and tips on how to spot them. Tip-offs include having to pay to get the job, a requirement to share credit card or bank account information, or the promise of access to otherwise private government jobs.

Other red flags are job postings with spelling errors, vague job descriptions, and limited information about the company and its address. Pushy interviewers who sound very urgent and press you to agree to the job *now* are another warning sign. And if you can't find information about people who work at the company on LinkedIn, be on the lookout for a scam.

If the gig seems too good to be true, it is. If anyone offers high pay for little work or extends an offer without even speaking with you, run the other way.

Three particularly dangerous job scams are jobs that require you to receive and send packages, jobs that require you to receive and transfer funds, and call center jobs that require you to sell a sham product or service and collect people's financial information. If you end up interviewing for a job that sounds like one of these, back out quickly.

Repackaging Scams

Some jobs offer you the chance to make a lot of money simply by receiving packages in the mail, repackaging them, and mailing them to other addresses. Sounds simple, right? And it is, until the police show up at your door and arrest you for trafficking drugs or stolen goods. These kinds of offers are particularly popular during the holiday season when they're sometimes described as work-from-home gift-wrapping jobs.

Just as you should never let anyone talk you into putting something in your suitcase for them at the airport, you should never let anyone bamboozle you into receiving and sending packages, especially if the details are vague and you cannot verify the contents. Jobs that ask you to do so are a big red flag. Get out as soon as you can and notify the Federal Trade Commission.

Money-Laundering Scams

Other jobs ask you to provide your banking information and then send you funds to deposit in your own account. They then transfer to another account later. Fake employers can spin all kinds of stories to make this seem legitimate, but if you're being asked to receive and transfer funds, you should stop immediately and look for another job. Chances are you're being enlisted as a money mule in a money-laundering operation.

Don't let anyone use you to transfer illegally obtained money from one fraud to another, obscuring their identities in the process and helping them evade authorities. This is another job that could easily land you in prison or, if you turn on your employer, in a witness protection program hiding away from the mob for years.

Even if you aren't being used as a money mule, you could end up a victim of theft. Some fake employers will send you a check for, say, $5,000 and then call to say they accidentally sent you too much and need you to mail back a check or money order for, say, $1,500. You mail $1,500 and deposit their $5,000 check only to find that their check bounces or is a fake.

Call Center Scams

In some call center jobs, the script you're asked to read from might make you feel a bit icky and set off alarm bells. If you feel uncomfortable, there's probably a good reason.

For example, you could find yourself convincing retirees that they are in grave danger of being defrauded or sued, and encouraging them to fork over large sums of money for legal protection or insurance or a membership in some or other protective club. Or you could find yourself persuading retirees to pay you a large sum to start an e-commerce business for them, promising to make them rich with little effort on their part.

If the goal in your call center job is to get a credit card number, expiration date, and CCV code based on spurious threats or promises, and hand those over to another part of the organization, you should leave immediately and alert the Federal Trade Commission. Many scams like this end up cleaning out people's bank accounts and causing untold misery for their victims. Participating in a scam like this can land you in a world of legal trouble.

Other Job-Related Scams

Here's a quick, and by no means comprehensive, list of other common scams you might run into while searching for a job:

- **The Bait and Switch:** At the interview, you find out the job you came in to discuss doesn't exist, but there is a much less desirable one available.
- **Career Consulting:** Someone asks to represent you in the job search but ends up selling you marketing, resume, and other services; this happens with so-called recruiters as well.

- **Crafts or Products Assembly:** Once you pay the enrollment fee, the company will send you items to assemble and pay you for them . . . if they are happy with your work. They won't be.
- **Dodgy Data Entry Jobs:** You get offered an exorbitant salary to perform a fairly simple data entry task—but first, you must pay out money in advance to receive training and materials.
- **Direct Deposit:** You provide an "employer" your bank info so they can deposit too-high-to-be-true paychecks; instead they empty your account.
- **Rebate Processor:** Unlike legitimate rebate-processing jobs, which require you to process forms administratively and pay a small amount for each form, rebate-processing scams require you to pay a training fee, post product ads online, and sell products for a small commission.
- **Shipping Jobs:** These will offer you the opportunity to work from home by repacking and mailing goods, which are likely stolen; if you get a check at all, it will be fake.
- **Stuffing Envelopes:** Companies have automated this process, so anyone offering to pay for it is hoping to encourage you to pay them for materials and recruit your friends into the scam.
- **Requests for Your Credit Report:** A potential employer asks you to provide your credit report or social security number so they can run a background check. They then use the information to steal your identity.
- **Unemployment Scams:** Services that offer to expedite your unemployment claims for a fee are often illegal, and won't get you your money any sooner than doing it yourself.

Think Twice Before You Apply to These Jobs

There are some jobs to which you should only apply with your eyes wide open because they are risky. So risky, in fact, that many people who sign up end up spending more than they earn.

Two of the most prevalent on job boards are multilevel marketing (MLM) jobs and lease—purchase truck-driving jobs.

Multilevel Marketing (MLM) Jobs

The first thing they told me is you don't need a social security number to sign into this business. You're going to be fine. It sounded like the perfect opportunity . . . I lost about $70,000. I kept moving forward because of my kids mostly and because I wanted to get some of that money back someday. I expected that, if I would go to a higher and higher level, maybe someday I would see a big check, one of those big checks they always promised you were going to get.

—Soledad M. in "The American Dream Denied: Herbalife Victims Speak Out"

MLM companies, also known as network marketing companies, include Amway™, Avon®, doTerra®, Herbalife, Mary Kay®, Scentsy, and many, many others.[13]

A major study by the AARP Foundation found that among the more than 20 million Americans who have participated in MLM companies, a full 74% have either lost money or made nothing at all.[14] In some particularly egregious cases, as many as 99% of the MLM participants have made less than the minimum wage.[15]

A close read of many MLM business earnings disclosures shows that even the top 1% of reps often earn less than $25,000 per year.[16] Be very wary of opportunities like this before leaping in.

The Promise

Here's how their pitch usually works.

You want to work from home, be your own boss, choose your own schedule, and earn unlimited amounts of money, right?

Well, the company will give you something extremely valuable—the opportunity to sell a popular and well-known brand of some product (be it beauty products, essential oils, knives, weight-loss shakes, or something else)—and to do so on your own terms.

How much you make will depend only on how hard you work. The sky's the limit. Work hard, and you could soon be debt-free, financially independent, even rich.

What could go wrong with that?

The Pitfalls

Well, here's the catch. Typically, you'll need to buy a supply of the products first. And then you'll need to sell them to your friends and family to earn a profit.

It turns out it is actually incredibly difficult to get your friends and families to buy enough essential oils or lipstick to make you rich. And if you spend all day every day badgering everyone in your contact list to buy the $500 makeup sets or Tupperware you're peddling, your friends will probably start cutting you off.

There are plenty of former reps and clients with horror stories, who were required to buy more inventory than they could realistically sell. Some were even encouraged to rent commercial properties and open stores or clubs at massive personal expense, and then buy enough inventory to stock the shelves.

The Pyramid

MLM companies encourage you not merely to sell the products, but to recruit friends and family to become salespeople themselves. And this is where the real earning opportunity lies, you'll be told, because in addition to earning a recruiting fee, you can also earn commissions on all future sales that your recruits make, and that their recruits make, and so on.

Imagine a lifetime of sitting back and earning a passive income from commissions and residuals?

MLMs follow a pyramid structure in which a few people at the top make lots of money off the sales commissions of recruits, while many at the bottom lose money. These companies rely more heavily on recruiting a steady stream of new salespeople than on attracting customers.

Critics charge that MLM businesses are no different from pyramid schemes, which are illegal. "Legitimate businesses make money selling products and services, not by recruiting. The drive to recruit, especially when coupled with deceptive and inflated income claims, is the hallmark of an illegal pyramid," warns Andrew Smith, director of the Bureau of Consumer Protection.

The Federal Trade Commission (FTC) warns people to be wary of MLM businesses and has charged several with deceiving distributors about their earning potential.

In 2016, for example, Herbalife, paid $200 million to settle FTC charges and was forced to restructure its US operations and compensate reps. In 2019, AdvoCare International, L.P. agreed to pay $150 million and be banned from the multi-level marketing business to resolve FTC charges that they were operating an illegal pyramid scheme.

The Prey

Despite information campaigns warning job seekers of their risks and multiple lawsuits alleging abuse, MLM businesses continue to grow.

Stay-at-home moms and dads, military wives and husbands, and semi-retirees: take special note. MLM businesses will recruit you aggressively, knowing that you desperately want financial independence paired with flexibility. Immigrants should also be cautious. MLM businesses promise you a path to the American dream. Some have reportedly appealed to immigrants without authorization to work in the United States by telling them they don't need a social security number to work as reps.

But remember my two rules: Don't fall for promises that are too good to be true, and think very, very carefully before you open your wallet. A job is supposed to pay you, not the other way around.

Lease-to-Own Truck-Operator Jobs

A lot of times, when I'm expecting to see a check for a couple of thousand dollars, I'm getting a bill for, like, $200 or $500 or $1,500.

—Kimberley Sikorski, discussing her experience with Prime Trucking on NPR's Planet Money podcast, August 14, 2020

Another kind of job opportunity that frequently causes workers to lose tens of thousands of dollars is lease–owner trucking.

Here's how it works.

The Pitch

You go through a truck-driver training program, and get paid a few hundred dollars a week just to be a student. This is great!

Upon completing the training program, you are offered a choice: Either be a salaried employee earning a modest wage . . . or be your own boss with—you guessed it—unlimited earning potential! All you have to do is sign up to buy your truck, which turns you into an owner–operator. At that point you command higher fees and set your own schedule because you own the truck.

Who would say "no" to doing the same job, but over time owning the truck they are driving? The trucking company makes this an even easier choice by offering you generous financing terms. Pay it off little by little each week. Sit back while the trucking company accountants register your LLC and take care of all the paperwork. Simple, right?

The Trouble

Here's the trouble. The costs quickly multiply—truck payments, insurance, gasoline, maintenance, parking. And they're deducted from your paycheck. So it's quite common to get negative paychecks or bills from the company after weeks of around-the-clock work. If you want any health or retirement benefits, you have to pay for those yourself as well.

This model is a great way for trucking companies to keep their costs low and have workers shoulder all the risk of doing business. But it's usually a terrible way for a truck driver to make a living.

Many earn less than minimum wage or even lose money and damage their credit scores in the process. And by many, I mean hundreds of thousands of Americans.

In fact, several trucking companies have paid millions to settle class-action lawsuits in which they were accused of misclassifying tens of thousands of employees or violating minimum wage laws. PAM Transport settled a suit for more than $16 million. Prime settled for $28 million. And Knight-Swift Transportation settled for $100 million.[17]

The Tragedy of the Lease–Owner Trap

The tragedy of the whole thing is that being a salaried company truck driver is actually a lucrative job.

Many long-haul trucking jobs pay $60,000 a year or more and provide generous benefits.

So don't be tricked into thinking that it's better to be your own boss and have your own company. It likely isn't. There are many benefits to being a regular employee with reliable paycheck and benefits, and the ability to give your two weeks' notice and move on to something else when the time is right.

Think twice before buying a $150,000, 20-ton truck of your own and being trapped by a truckload of debt.

Summary

- ☐ When racing against the robots, apply within two days of a new job posting.
- ☐ Don't self-disqualify; apply to roles where you meet 40% or more of the requirements.
- ☐ Make it personal; apply to places where you know people, love the product, or live close by.
- ☐ Read public reviews from people within the company to get a sense of culture and fit.
- ☐ Many great opportunities require only weeks of training in a single skill. Research emerging job categories to get in while demand is high.
- ☐ Consider freelancing to gain experience, build up a portfolio of projects, and cultivate references.
- ☐ Be suspicious of jobs that sound too good to be true or that require you to spend thousands of dollars before you earn.

How to Ace a Pre-Screen

> *"I got a call back for a job while cooking, and ran outside to get away from my barking dogs. I had the phone, a knife, and a potato. I told the employer: 'Sorry, sorry, hold on! I'm carving your number onto a potato.' Still got the job!"*
>
> —*Employee with great knife skills*

Congratulations! You have heard back from a potential employer—maybe several potential employers—so the next step is the interview, right? Not always. At many companies you still have one more hurdle to overcome before you're sitting face-to-face with someone who has the power to hire you. Welcome to the pre-screen!

A lot of employers will pre-screen you before bringing you in for an interview. Usually done by phone, a pre-screen is fundamentally a verification exercise. Do you exist? Do you sound credible? Will you verbally affirm the same things you said on your resume.

The phone screen is frequently done by a recruiter versus the actual hiring manager. This is *not* an interview. In fact, the way you know the phone screen went well is if after it's over, you're scheduling the *actual* interview.

It is dead simple to get past this step. Yet for many, this is where their application stops. Here's how to navigate the phone screen hurdle.

> *"A lot of people are smart and put some of the language from our job descriptions directly into their resume. Others, however, take it too far. One candidate tried to jam our entire job description into the details of his work experience for his last job. During the phone screen my suspicions were quickly confirmed. He couldn't even remember the things he'd listed. Needless to say, he didn't get the job."*
>
> —Recruiter who sees what you're up to

Read Your Email and Answer Your *&#%* Phone

Here's a fact that works to your advantage: As many as 75% of candidates who apply to a job don't answer when the recruiter reaches out.[1] Employers *hate* it when they can't get in touch with you. You have an edge in the job market today just by showing common courtesy. (Sadly, this is what constitutes real advice in the modern job-seeking marketplace.)

Once you've applied to a job, check your email regularly and have your phone on you. Take every call—even if your caller ID marks the call "Unknown."

That's it. That's all you have to do to give yourself a better shot at success. I understand you might be reluctant to answer phone calls from numbers you don't recognize. Unfortunately, that's a risk you have to take—until you have the job. And if you miss a call, don't be afraid to call back. Once you have been hired, you can feel free to ignore those spam calls again.

Speaking of spam, make sure you check the spam folder on your email. If you're receiving messages from a company for the first time, that's sometimes where the email algorithm will put them. If you don't check your spam regularly, those emails will sit unopened.

> *"I left three voicemail messages for a candidate before taking him out of the running. A month later, he returned my call asking for the interview. I decided to have some fun and tell him*

> *that, in the time since I had left the message, we had already filled the job, promoted the person, and hired a second person to fill his shoes."*
>
> *—Employer with a sadistic sense of fun*

This Is *Not* the Time to Ask Questions

These calls are in most cases formulaic exercises in confirming your key skills and work history. This is not a time for expanded color commentary and it is *especially* not the time to start sharing any insecurities you might have. Normally those insecurities will manifest in the form of you asking questions.

Example:

Phone screener: "Do you have more than a year of experience working with Software X?"

Correct answer: "Yes I do.

Incorrect answer: "Well I have used the software for over a year, but only these components. Does Software play a big part in this role?"

It's Okay to Be Excited

Enthusiasm during a job search always helps you. And it's always persuasive to the person on the other end of the conversation, even if all they are doing is checking some boxes. There are several basic strategies to convey enthusiasm.

Smile When You Talk

When you smile, you make yourself happier—even when you aren't.[2] The simple act of smiling releases feel-good hormones, which help relax your body, plus lower your heart rate and blood pressure. Smiling is a performance-enhancing drug for hitting a home run on a pre-screen.

And it doesn't just help you. A smile puts everyone in the conversation at ease—even over the phone! Researchers have seen that people on the other end of a phone conversation can actually *hear* your smile.[3] They can even tell when you're giving off a genuine, or "Duchenne," smile, which is contagious! And when your interviewer smiles, they're getting that same performance-enhancing feeling that you are. Maya Angelou said, "People will forget what you did, but people will never forget how you made them feel." She must have done a lot of pre-screens.

Stand Up

One common technique is to stand up. That might sound strange, because the person on the other end of the phone can't see you. But when you stand up during a sales call or a pre-screen, you can draw on the energy of your entire body to sound more convincing or convey enthusiasm. Pacing is also a great way to burn off nervous energy.

Be Prepared

Don't underestimate the power of visualization. You can't know exactly what an employer will ask you during a pre-screen, but you can think through what the conversation might sound like.

Look over the job posting to which you responded. Think about what the company says it is looking for, and the questions it wants applicants to answer. Those are the questions that are likely to come up during a pre-screen. Write them down, and practice answering them—simply. It won't take much effort to prepare for a pre-screen, but a few minutes of mental practice reps can make a big difference in showing the screener you're ready to meet the real judges.

The good news is that in a pre-screen interview, half of the sales work is already done. You know that the employer is interested: that's why they're on the phone with you. So you don't have to make a "hard sell." Just be confident in your brand—and get ready to move on to the next stage in your job search plan.

"It's so easy to pass a pre-screen interview, but so many people screw it up. They forget the job they applied for, or have no idea what the job responsibilities are, or the answers they give don't match up with what their resume says. If you're applying for lots of jobs, the best advice I can give you is to make sure you keep good notes on the jobs you applied for and the basic responsibilities of each one. And keep those notes with you at all times in case you get a call and need to access them quickly. It's a shame to lose out on a job opportunity just because you fail to do a tiny bit of planning."

—Employer who wishes you'd pay more attention

Summary

- ☐ Keep your email and phone nearby so you're ready to talk when a company reaches out.
- ☐ Your first "interview" could be a pre-screen; keep the conversation very high level.
- ☐ Share your enthusiasm and be prepared.

9 What to Wear to an Interview

"I bought a new suit before doing a day of interviews at a company I was dying to get into. The interviews went great and we finished after almost four hours. I left and later realized the price tag on my jacket was still attached the entire time."

— *Mortified job seeker*

The average job interview is between 30 and 60 minutes.

According to research done at the University of Oregon, how long do you think it takes for an interviewer to decide whether you're hireable?[1]

a. 15 minutes
b. 30 minutes
c. 45 minutes
d. 60 minutes

The correct answer is "none of the above." You get 20 seconds.

In the first 20 seconds, your interviewer will reach numerous judgments about you, which are unlikely to change regardless of how long they speak with you. Those judgments will include your competence, warmth, and hireability.

First impressions are critically important in an interview—arguably more important than most of what you will do or say over the next 60 minutes. What the interviewer sees in the first 20 seconds—your clothes and demeanor—will play a HUGE role in whether you win the job. We'll cover how to evoke the right demeanor in the next chapter, but first let's focus on your clothes.

Understand the Unconscious Bias Around Apparel

"I work at a bank. It doesn't take a lot of research to find out the proper outfit for employees of banks. And yet, I've had people walk in for interviews dressed in blue jeans, or wearing moccasins, and I've told them straight up that I wasn't going to hire them because of their lack of professional attire. I've also had candidates come in wearing wrinkled shirts, inappropriately short skirts, and one time, a Christmas sweater in October. I don't understand what these people are thinking."

—Employer who is not a fan of business casual

Research has shown that people who wear nice clothing get judged as more competent. In a study conducted by researchers at Princeton University, test subjects were given pictures of faces and asked to rate their competence.[2] The catch, however, was that all the faces were attached to different upper-body clothing. Faces attached to clothing perceived as "more expensive" by an observer—whether it was a T-shirt, sweater, or other top—led to higher competence ratings of the person pictured than similar clothes judged as "cheaper."

Even worse, to the dismay of the researchers, when they explicitly told the test subjects to ignore the clothing in their ratings, they still scored the pictures of people in "more expensive" clothing as more competent. The unconscious bias was so strong that even when made aware of it, the participants could not turn it off.

Does this mean you need to spend a lot of money on clothes for your interview? No. Fortunately, with the explosion of fast fashion retail (H&M, Zara, Forever 21, etcetera) looking stylish has never been more affordable.

Just remember that you *will* be judged by what you choose to wear, and if you've gotten all the way to an in-person interview, buying a new outfit is an investment that can pay off big time.

An important note here: If you buy new clothing, invest in an iron. You do not want your interviewer to believe this is the first time you've ever tried to look nice. Men's dress shirts in particular are folded when packaged. This leaves distinct "right out of the wrapper" creases that are a clear tell that dressing nicely is something you're only dabbling in. Remember that every time an interviewer notices details, you run the risk of triggering their bias.

> *"When a person walks in the door for an interview I can tell in seconds whether or not they have a chance. Just seeing how they dressed, the way they carry themselves, and their anxiety level tells me a lot about them before we even start talking."*
>
> —*Employer who has already started the interview*

Picking Your Interview Outfit

HOW TO PICK THE RIGHT INTERVIEW OUTFIT

Obviously not all jobs have the same dress code. It's a very different thing to interview at a retail clothing store than it is to interview at an accounting office. There is no one-size-fits-all outfit that works for every interview, *but* there is a simple truth you can apply to be sure you're always dressed for success: If you think your outfit looks good, then you *do* look good.

Scientists call this "enclothed cognition."[3] The outfit you wear has the power to change your posture, boost your confidence, and heighten your mood. Here's how to find the outfit that triggers your best self.

Put this book down, grab a notebook, and head to a public space. Sip a cup of your preferred beverage, and start doing some serious people watching. As people pass, your challenge is to label them with a single adjective. Are they sloppy? Casual? Slick? Grungy? The point of the exercise is you *only* get one word, and you have to label them in the few seconds they take to walk by.

Now I want you to pay special attention to people who you would label with an adjective that matches how you'd want an interviewer to label you. We're talking about any of the following:

1. Polished
2. Professional
3. Confident
4. Trustworthy
5. Stylish
6. Presentable

Write down the adjective you selected and then document what those people are wearing. The key thing here is to note the details. Hair, shoes, belts, accessories—log it all! See if a pattern emerges.

Stylists tell me that people tend to be impressed by patternless navy blue outfits that are fitted and tucked in. (That may be why police officers and firemen wear blue uniforms.) But hey, go with whatever jumps out at you. The important part is to identify the style that has positive associations, and then to go out and buy that outfit!

Once you do buy that outfit, unless you are 100% confident in your fashion sense (and I speak from personal experience when I say that only 1% of us should be 100% confident), form a fashion-police focus group of two or three friends whom you can trust to give their honest feedback about the professionalism and appropriateness of your outfit. And promise me that if there's a unanimous veto of your outfit, trust the wisdom of your friends, return the outfit, and try again.

How You Know Your Interview Outfit Is Right

I guarantee if we put you in a Superman or Wonder Woman costume, you would naturally set your shoulders back, puff out your chest, and put your fists on your hips. Scientists refer to this as a "Power Pose." A good interview outfit will trigger the same posture!

Keep trying on different outfits until you fall into that position reflexively. When you look in the mirror are you instinctively stiffening your spine and thrusting your chest forward? Are you spinning around to see if it looks as good from all sides? Do you feel like you can hardly recognize yourself? Power posing is our natural reaction when our brain tells us we're

YOU KNOW YOUR OUTFIT IS RIGHT WHEN YOU POWER POSE

looking good! The right interview outfit will trigger changes in how you carry yourself that other people will notice. Keep shopping until you find an outfit that makes you want to kick ass!

Perfume and Cologne Are a *Definite* No

Let me hit you with some science. According to the 1,000 genomes project,[4] there are 400 genes involved in your sense of smell and more than 900,000 different presentations of those genes. Because of this wide genetic variability, on average, there is a 30% difference in how any two people respond to the same scent. To put it simply, perfume that smells good to you is another person's cloying floral compost pile.

Smell also triggers memories that are clearer, more intense, and more emotional, according to research from the University of Toronto.[5] What memories will the scent you're wearing trigger? You have no idea!

Remember, we're trying to hack your interviewer's biases. That means controlling every part of what you present to them. You might think coconut makes you smell tropical. For your interviewer it's a crushing reminder of their bad break up.

Make sure the defining thing your interviewer remembers about you is *not* how you smell. Go to every interview scentless. No perfume, cologne, aftershave, baby powder, body lotion, or scented hair spray.

"We had a candidate that everybody absolutely loved! Except for one thing. Each and every person that interviewed him independently reported that the cologne he was wearing was so strong it would be impossible to work with him. Hoping it was a one-time mistake, I asked him back a week later for a second round of interviews, but the strong cologne returned with him. The team and I talked about offering him the job contingent on him not wearing cologne, but for some the cologne was a red flag. They felt if he was so unaware of his impact on those around him, what else would he be unaware about? He has no idea he lost the job solely because of the cologne he used."

—Employer with a nose for talent

Let's Talk About Sweat

When I interview I get really sweaty hands. I try to wipe them off on my pants but you never get it all. The guy interviewing me apparently had the same problem because when we shook hands at the end our sweaty hands cupping together made a loud fart noise. Didn't get the job.

11:31 AM • Nov 1, 2020 • Twitter for iPhone

It's unfair, but when you sweat, others view you as less confident, less competent, and less trustworthy.[6] We can't stop you from sweating, but we *can* help you cover it up much better than you have been. Here are some simple tips to keep you cool and dry:

1. Wear antiperspirant (not just deodorant). If you're someone with serious sweat issues, you may want to talk to a doctor about a prescription strength option.
2. Wear a cotton or sweat-proof undershirt.
3. Use sweat pads. Sweat pads are sweat-capturing products that attach directly to your underarms or under your clothes. Think of it like an armpit diaper.
4. Bring a kerchief or scarf (thank you modern acceptable fashion choice) and use it to keep your hands dry.
5. Ask for a cup of ice water before the interview, wrap a napkin around it, and hold it with your right hand to keep your hand cool.
6. Don't drink alcohol the night before your interview, and avoid caffeine the day of the interview. Both can trigger increased sweating.[7]
7. Wear clothing items that don't show sweat, and consider investing in a sweat-proof undershirt. Blazers are great for hiding armpit sweat patches.

Summary

☐ You've got 20 seconds or less to make a good impression.
☐ The right outfit is one that *you* think you look good in.
☐ Avoid wearing scents and control your sweat.

10 How to Ace a Job Interview

"I asked an engineering candidate why he wanted to leave his current job. His response revealed a lot: 'There are 12 people who share an air conditioning zone in our office. Every day the thermostat is set to an uncomfortably warm temperature and I am prohibited by the others from turning it down.' This guy was a brilliant software developer, but he was obviously a little odd. We hired him and gave him his own office."

—*Employer willing to make accommodations*

If interviews make you nervous, let me assure you that you're not alone. A full 93% of job seekers feel nervous about interviewing.[1] It's so common that a lot of training time for interviewers is spent on how to put the interviewee at ease.

However, the fear your competition feels about interviewing is about to become your advantage! I'm going to give you the key to staying calm from beginning to end and, what's more, make a standout impact with whoever conducts the interview.

Don't Die in the First 20 Seconds ━━━━

THE FIRST IMPRESSION IS THE ONLY IMPRESSION YOU GET

Earlier, I shared the research that shows told you that your interviewer leaps to a conclusion about your hireability in the first 20 seconds, and that their first impression of you will be incredibly difficult to change. While you can't win the job in the first 20 seconds, you certainly can lose it.

Armed with that knowledge, you already put on an outfit that makes you feel confident. Now you're going to control their first impression. Ready?

Here are the four things you're going to do as soon as you meet your interviewer:

Give a *Real* Smile

Did you know that humans can detect the difference between a real smile and a fake one? Fake smiles happen only with your mouth. A real smile (or *Duchenne* smile) is defined by contraction of the muscles around the mouth *and* the eyes.

You are going to find a way to offer a *real* smile. I don't care if you have to practice in a mirror, think about your favorite comedy, or just repeat in your head "crinkle my eyes, crinkle my eyes!" Somehow you are going to project happiness. Why?

Research tells us that people are treated differently when they offer genuine smiles. One study showed that the more a person smiled, the more people expected an interaction with that person to go well.[2]

But smiling does more than bias people positively toward you; it also calms you down. Like deep breaths, smiling reduces stress hormones in your bloodstream. It is literally putting both you and your interviewer at ease.

Make Strong Eye Contact

As soon as your interviewer walks into the room give them a real smile *and make strong eye contact.*

Making eye contact does multiple things to the brain of the person interviewing you. It heightens their perception of your confidence,[3] elevates your perceived social status, increases their belief in what you have to say, and triggers multiple parts of the brain involved in empathy.[4] This all means your interviewer will be primed to connect with you.

Important note: I only want you to make great eye contact at the start! After that first conscious use of eye contact, go back to your normal eye contact pattern. Making too much eye contact in conversation signals that you are trying to sell something, which is sometimes associated with dishonesty.[5]

"I interviewed a candidate who didn't make eye contact with me once during the entire interview. He kept his head down, looking at the table or the wall, the whole time. This was for a job in sales!"

—Employer who told this story while making eye contact

Offer a Firm Handshake

A good handshake is another easy way to create a positive perception of yourself. A good handshake signals confidence and extraversion.

So whether you meet the interviewer in the waiting area, or later in the meeting room, you're going to hack their brain by giving them a real smile, looking them in the eye, and offering a firm handshake.

> *"If anybody gives me a dead fish handshake, they're automatically ruled out. I just can't have anybody on my team who doesn't have a firm handshake."*
>
> —*Employer and handshake evaluator*

Say the Name of Your Interviewer

Your final instruction to cement those first 20 seconds is the easiest, most natural thing in the world—speak the name of the person interviewing you immediately.

Why are you doing this?

Humans *love* being addressed by name. We view it as a compliment to have our names remembered.[6] It is also seen as a sign of respect. By speaking their names, you are demonstrating to the interviewer that you see them, specifically, and that they are important. You're also creating an increased feeling of familiarity so that you relax as the interview begins.

The key thing here is *remembering* the person's name. You're going to use it again later on with powerful effect to make sure the interview gets off to a great start. So bring a pad and a pen to write their name down if you have to, but make sure you know the name of your interviewer.

> *"To help remember names, I typically make a point of saying the person's name three times early on in the conversation when meeting new people. And when I'm interviewing for a job, I'm even more careful to do it. In my last interview, I worked in the interviewer's name three times, and then at the*

end, I thanked Janice for her time. Except her name was Alice. I wasn't surprised when I didn't get the job."

—Job seeker who tried

Summary

1. Smile.
2. Make strong eye contact.
3. Offer a firm handshake.
4. Say their name.

How to Crush the Next 29 Minutes and 40 Seconds of the Interview

Congratulations. You made a standout first impression. Everything is going your way. However, now comes the trap. Across every job category and every level of seniority, the most frequently asked opening question in a job interview is:

Tell me about yourself . . .

Let me promise you something. No one *ever* wants you to really answer this question. In fact, if there is a golden rule of interviewing it's simply this; talk about them more than you talk about you.

The interviewer has already read your resume. They don't need you to verbally walk them through it. They don't need you to guess what lower-level details might be interesting to them. No. If you get this question, you are going to pivot immediately.

"I once opened up an interview asking the candidate to 'tell me about yourself' and he went on for the entire 30 minutes without stopping."

—Interviewer still waiting for his turn

The Magical First Sentence

USE THE MAGICAL FIRST SENTENCE

In the last section I told you we were going to use the name of your interviewer one more time. Well, the moment is here. It's time for you to learn the magical first sentence.

This sentence is your powerhouse opening to kick off what will be a great interview! (And it doesn't matter what their opening question is—it works for every possible question.) Ready to memorize a sentence? Here you go:

"[INSERT INTERVIEWER NAME]—(*one-second pause*)—I'm so excited to be here because [fill in the blank with something specific about the business]."

Some examples to show you how the sentence works in a real interview situation:

Interviewer: "So . . . tell me about yourself."

"Brian, I am so excited to be here because I have spent the last ten years building marketing strategies, and what you folks do to build a brand is beyond anything I've ever seen. How did you get the idea to advertise on podcasts? It's brilliant!"

"Margaret, I am so excited to be here because I love your product. I bet everyone here feels lucky to work on a product that is so easy to stand behind."

"Ms. Jones, I am so excited to be here because I love great service, and I have personally experienced great service here as a customer. Is that something you train or is it just the kind of person you hire?"

"Jane, I am so excited to be here. This would be my first job out of college. I've read all about your leadership team online. They are next-level! How did this company attract so much talent?!"

"Mr. Duncan, I am so excited to be here. After two tours in the military, I put a premium on operational excellence, and from what I've read online you pride yourselves on getting the details right and accountability. That's uncommon these days. How do you maintain that culture here?"

Let's break down the reasons it works:

1. Using a person's name spikes their attention. It's an uncontrollable response in the brain that puts them at maximum focus on what you say next.
2. Expressing interest is incredibly powerful. One of the most replicated findings in social psychology is that people like people who like them first. It is called "reciprocal liking." This proves true in dating, social groups, and job interviews.
3. Even though they've asked you to "tell me about yourself" you've immediately pivoted the conversation back to talking about them! Harvard neuroscientists tell us people like talking about themselves so much it's almost impossible for them to resist.[7] It triggers the same sensation of pleasure in our brain as food, money, or even sex!
4. To make the magical first sentence work, you actually have to do some research on the company. Only two in three candidates will do that research.[8] But if you *really* want to stand out, know that fewer

than one in five candidates will research the interviewer themselves.[9] Asking a question about your interviewer is the black-belt level use of the magical first sentence!

"Jon, I am so excited to be here. I was already excited about the company, but when I read your background I was excited to meet you. You've worked at some incredible companies in the past. How does this company stack up"

"Erica, I am so excited to be here. I am a fan of your service! I actually saw a video online of you talking about the product. Your passion was contagious! How do you stay so calm on camera?!"

You know the magical first sentence worked if your interviewer immediately starts talking. There are fireworks going off in their brain. This is *the best possible start to an interview*. Once you've triggered the endorphin response, it's easy to keep it going.

> *"I put a lot of weight on how enthusiastic a candidate is during the interview. Why? Because it's easy to tell how enthusiastic a candidate is about the job by observing how enthusiastic they are during the interview. Anybody who can't even get excited during an interview certainly isn't going to be excited about the job after a few months."*
>
> —*Employer who does not want you to curb your enthusiasm*

Hit the Ball Back Every Time

Great interviews are when the two parties spend an *equal* amount of time talking. Think of a tennis match versus bowling. Your interviewer is *not* there to set up pins so you can knock them down. They are trying to figure out what it would be like to work with you. They learn more from how well you listen, what questions you ask, and how you process new information than they do from listening to you talk about yourself. Fully 93% of employers rate "soft skills" as essential in a hiring decision.[10]

Your goal is to start conversations, not deliver monologues. Once you've used the magic sentence up front, the conversation has already started. Now you just need to make a game of ending every answer you give with a question. In essence, after everything you say—I want you to "hit the ball back."

Interviewer: "What were your day-to-day responsibilities at Company X?"

Candidate: "I would make copies, answer phones, and manage my supervisor's calendar. But I took pride in looking for ways to enhance our department culture. I organized team-building events and holiday contests. **Do you do any sort of team building here?"**

Candidate: "I was an intern so I spent a lot of time as an observer in meetings. The biggest thing I did was write up meeting minutes to document decisions. **How do you keep everyone on the same page here?"**

> **"You can usually tell a lot more about a person from the questions they ask than from the answers they give."**
>
> **—Employer who wants to hear your questions**

Standing Out

One of the things people fail to appreciate in an interview is that you aren't just trying to prove you can do the job, you're trying to prove you can do the job better than all the other candidates you're competing against. This is not a test you have to pass; it's a contest with only *one* winner.

You can wear the right outfit, project the just-right image, and have a great conversation, but at the end of the interview there is one thing that the best candidates do to cement their status as top pick: create a memorable moment.

But what is a memorable moment and how do you create it? It's simple really. A memorable moment is when the interviewer feels like *they* have been heard. I'm talking about a moment where the interviewer feels like they've taught you something, made you change your mind, or taken an idea you brought in with you and made it better.

You want your interviewer to *know* that you have respect for them and their ideas. You want to show rather than tell them that you will be a pleasure to work with. So now that you understand the goal, how do you get to this moment?

How to Create a Memorable Moment

The key thing to understand about human psychology is that your interviewer is more likely to remember you if they feel like *they* did well in the interview. Great answers to interview questions will make you a final candidate, but what gets you the job is when your interviewer doesn't just rate you as qualified, but actually wants to work with you.

So how do you make your interviewer feel great? I encourage you to practice the two-second pause. When your interviewer asks you a question, or makes a point in a back-and-forth dialogue, take a full two seconds before responding.

In the normal flow of conversation, people speak rapidly, often interrupting each other before sentences are fully complete. It doesn't sound like a long time, but breaks in conversation of two seconds are so uncommon they stand out. Show them you're thinking about what they said or the question they asked. Not only will it make prepared answers feel more authentic, but you're highlighting that you're a thoughtful listener. And listening is a superpower. Everyone loves a great listener.

"I Have a Story to Tell You . . ."

Want to be *really* memorable? Tell stories. Multiple studies have shown that stories are associated with increased recall and better comprehension.[11] In fact, those studies have shown that facts are 20 times more likely to be remembered if they're part of a story. That's 20 *times* more likely, not 20 *percent* more likely. That's huge.[12]

Pretend for a second that you and I just had a conversation and covered three topics.

Topic 1: "The features of my new car."

Topic 2: "The most embarrassing thing that ever happened to me."

Topic 3: "Places I went on my vacation."

Which part of our conversation do you think you'll remember a month from now? Your goal in every interview is to be memorable. If you ever find yourself rattling off a list, let me assure you that you are boring your interviewer. *No one* cares about lists.

Interviewers are asking you questions in the hopes of starting a conversation. Nothing captures attention and makes a person want to share back more than a good story. *Always* tell stories. (Test it out at home! Tell someone how you got a scar on your body. See if the conversation ends without them telling you a story about their own scars.)

Even if it seems impossible to answer with a story, you're going to force one in there. And your greatest tool for doing so is this sentence:

"I have a story to tell you . . ."

Compare and contrast what happens when you answer a question with a story.

Interviewer: What were your day-to-day responsibilities at Company X?

Answer: I answered phones, filed documents, made copies, and fetched coffee.

Answer: I answered phones, filed documents, made copies, and fetched coffee. But oh do I have a story to tell you! I did one thing that completely blew up (in a good way). I noticed the team was mostly eating lunch at their desks. One Friday, I ordered pizza for the office as a surprise. When I sent out the email, there was a stampede! I learned that no matter how much they are paid, if you tell people there is free, lukewarm pizza in the kitchen, the team will not only wait in line to get it, but sit down and eat a meal together. My boss loved it and Pizza Fridays were born. It literally became a selling point in our recruiting! Do you do any kind of team building here?

Storytelling can take practice. Challenge yourself to rehearse at least two stories so you have them in your back pocket when you go into the interview. Ideally, pick narratives where the moral of the story is something you learned. You want to show (versus tell) that you're capable of personal growth.

> *"I rarely take notes. Good candidates get me excited. I always remember them and the moment they sold me. I'll share that moment when I sell others internally on why we should bring the candidate on board."*
>
> —Employer who doesn't bring a notepad to an interview

Be Ready for These Common Interview Questions

After "tell me about yourself," there are two other questions that trip up job seekers more than the rest. Go in prepared to handle these.

"Why Are You Looking to Leave Your Current Job?"

Trap alert! Trap alert! There is no answer you can give to this question that meaningfully increases your chances of getting hired. There is, however, one answer that is *definitely* wrong. All of the following are professionally acceptable answers:

- I want to be at a [fill in the blank] company. (Larger, smaller, faster paced, etc.).
- The commute is killing me.
- There is no promotion path available to me.
- I am looking for a place where I can learn new things.
- I want to make more money.

The wrong answer? *Anything* negative about the last boss you worked for, or worse, the company itself.

Promise yourself right now that you will never speak ill of your current or last employer. No matter how valid your complaint, denigrating your current or previous employer, will always reflect poorly on you. This goes double if you're early in your career.

The further you get into your career the more you'll realize there are two sides to every story. Experienced hiring managers won't swallow what you tell them whole. When someone is unhappy at a job, the mature thing is to leave. Congratulations, you're doing the mature thing! Never make it personal.

"How Much Are You Looking to Get Paid?"

> *"The best answer I ever got to the question, 'How much do you want to get paid?' was from a woman who, handed me a printed salary study. She said 'I did research online and the average salary range for this job is $40,000 –$60,000, but I'm above-average. Given my proven track record, I want $70,000.' I learned more about her from her answer to that question than any other I asked in the interview."*
>
> —*Employer who wished they researched their own salary better*

Employers love to sneak this question in there. It's one of the five most commonly asked interview questions. Don't get caught flat-footed.

If you don't already have a specific salary target in mind (and in most cases, even if you do) do your research online and know the market rate for the role. It's important to remember that the answer to this question is *not* whatever your last job paid plus a slight bump. The answer to this question is what the market will bear! To find out what that is just go to: www .ziprecruiter.com/Salaries.

At the ZipRecruiter salary page you can see what employers in your market are *actually* paying for the role, based on payroll data, salaries listed in job postings, and official government data.

Some negotiating pros will tell you to "never name a number first." I'd argue it's fine to give a number if you know what you need, but you are also safe going with something like this:

Of course I want to get paid a fair market rate, but there are many factors in how I view the question. The opportunity to learn, opportunity to advance, the people I get to work with, and what I get to work on are all important considerations.

"Do You Have Any Questions?" Yes, You Do!

"The most telling part of the interview for me is when I ask the candidate, 'Do you have any questions for me?' If they have none or ask run-of-the-mill questions, it's a fail. I want to feel like they are genuinely curious. When they make me feel like they're actually interviewing me, they get major points in my book."

—*Employer who is bored by most questions*

Always have questions at the end.

Asking questions (and the quality of the questions you ask) is one more way to *show* versus *tell* the interviewer what it will be like to work with you. You want to show that you're thoughtful about the business, care about culture, and, most importantly, that you are interested.

The right questions also give an interviewer the chance to talk more about themselves, which we know from earlier makes them like you more. Best of all, it puts them in a position where they are trying to sell *you* on the company. The more time they invest in you, the more they'll feel like you're already part of their team.

Here are some great questions you can ask:

- What gets you excited about working here?
- What have you learned about being successful here?
- What are some of the challenges you've experienced here?
- If I joined the team, who do you think would be most helpful in bringing me up to speed?
- How would you envision my first month here versus my sixth month?
- What are you most proud of from the work you have done here?
- Do you have any hesitations about why I may not be the right fit?

That last one may feel awkward, but the discussion it generates is a great way to address any questions they might have about hiring you head on.

"Why Do You Want to Work at This Company?"

Make sure that your answer is specific to this company and this job—and shows you've done your homework. You can discuss what about this company intrigues you, how you've seen it evolve, what excites you about the future, and your hope to help it get there. It never hurts to sprinkle in some compliments about the other employees you've met so far and how they've increased your enthusiasm.

"What Are Your Greatest Strengths/Weaknesses?"

The most overused interview question in history. For a response that will stick with the interviewer, choose just one or two strengths and back them up with stories and stats. On the weakness side, mention something that would not directly impact your day-to-day performance (if it's a data-heavy role, talk about public speaking), and lay out the steps you've taken to improve.

"Tell Me About a Work Conflict and How You Dealt with It."

This is a thorny one. What your interviewer is trying to assess is how you deal with challenges within a team. Don't shy away from admitting you've had conflicts. We all do—and saying you haven't is insincere. Briefly lay out the issue, then pivot to how you dealt with it and grew.

"What's Your Management Style?"

"There are only two types of bosses in the world. Those you work with, and those you work for." That's your opening line! Fill in the rest with an explanation of which you are and why. Again, make sure to tell stories. You want to *show* them how you manage rather than tell them. I recommend telling at least one story about a good day, and at least one story about a bad one.

"What Do You Do When You're Not at Work?"

This is a great question! It's a way to share your passions on a more personal level. If you researched your interviewer (which, of course you did!) you may have found out about a passion of theirs that you are excited about too. If not, talk about the things that get you excited. Bonus points if you connect it to the job. One thing to keep in mind: Don't make it sound like it takes up too much of your time, or they may wonder about your willingness to put the time in at the office.

"Where Do You See Yourself in Five Years?"

Another cliche. What they're really trying to figure out is how you plan long term and if your goals align with the company and role. Talk about how the work you'll be doing in this new role would contribute to where you'd ultimately like to go. Watch out for sounding too eager; it may seem as though you don't intend on sticking around for too long, or will soon be pestering them for a promotion.

"What Would Your 30/60/90 Plan Be?"

This is a way for your potential boss to get a sense of how you'd approach the first/second/third month of your new job. Obviously, you won't really know what's needed until you start, but they want to see how you'd go about assessing the situation. A good rule is to talk about how you'd take the time to talk to the right people and understand what's needed before ruffling feathers by causing upheaval to the status quo.

"How Many Bathroom Stalls Are There in a New York City Skyscraper?"

Make sure you look this answer up and memorize it! I'm kidding. It's a ridiculous question. On purpose. What the interviewer is really trying to get at with questions like this is seeing how you respond under pressure and how you methodically think through complex questions. Feel free to jump up on the meeting room whiteboard or grab a piece of paper and talk through how you'd go about figuring this one out.

How to Be Awesome in a Video Interview

"I had an automated video interview in which the computer would ask a question and give you 30 seconds to record a video

of your answer. For one of the questions, I had no idea what to say for an answer, so I just stood there as still as could be without blinking for 30 seconds, so they thought the video had a glitch and froze up. Still got the job."

—Employee who nailed the video interview

In a postpandemic world, video interviewing has burst onto the scene, and is certain to be a fixture in the future of work.

Remember how I said you have 20 seconds to make a first impression? Video interviewing changes the time frame. Now you get one second. You heard me—one second.

In a series of experiments at Princeton University,[13] researchers determined that human beings make several judgments about another person's character from observing their face for less than one second. Included in those judgments are attractiveness, likeability, trustworthiness, aggressiveness, and most importantly—competence.

Before the idea of having only one second triggers your anxiety, let me explain why this is *awesome* for you. Unlike when you go in for an in-person interview, you have 100% control over what your interviewer sees in the first second they meet you. You can stage every detail to make sure they see the very best version of who you are—or at least the parts of you that you want them to see. And the confidence-boosting part is you can test it out over and over before you jump on the call.

Video Interview Checklist

"Haven't we all heard enough stories by now of people getting caught on Zoom in their underwear? I shouldn't have to say this but, if you're going to be on video—WEAR PANTS! This is not the area of your life in which you want to cut corners. It only takes five seconds to put on a pair of pants, people!"

—Pants-wearing employer

Here's your checklist to make sure you own every part of your first impression.

Overgroom

Hi-resolution retina displays on modern phones and computers are amazing. However, they have a downside; an interviewer can see your face on a Zoom call with close up, real-world quality. Here are some simple grooming tips to navigate the "extreme clarity" of today's screens:

1. Select solid color outfits. No stripes or patterns. No denim. Remember, you want the clothes to look "richer." Dark colors are a safer bet.
2. Use a styling product to hold your hair in place. No stray hairs to distract your interviewer.
3. For men, shave your face, or brush your beard. We don't want stray hairs coming out the side of your face either.
4. For women (or long-haired men), if your hair is long enough, consider a ponytail.
5. Makeup is your friend (for either gender), to cover up blemishes or bags under your eyes. The point of the makeup is to keep the attention on what you're saying. Don't overdo it. Your words are the star of this show.
6. Clean your glasses.
7. Wear pants. You never know if you'll have to stand up.
8. Check your eyebrows. You don't want hairy caterpillars crawling across your face. Cut them, pluck them, or smooth them down.
9. Zoom offers a setting called "Touch up my appearance," which applies a subtle filter to make you look better. Accept their kind offer.

Pick a Spot With Good Light

Here is a hierarchy from "best" to "worst" for lighting options.

1. Natural light. Sit facing a window so that your face is lit by the sun. (Sitting with your back to the window will have a darkening effect and make it hard to see you.)
2. Sitting outside in the sunlight is a great option if you can find a quiet space. No dogs barking, street traffic, or kids playing. Make sure your face is toward the sun and that your background isn't facing the garbage cans.
3. "Artificial lighting" makes it sound like you have to call in a Hollywood production crew, but it really doesn't take much. It isn't crazy to invest in a ring light. This is a small bright light that rests beside or on top of

your computer. You can find them online, starting around $30. You can also try taking a desk lamp you already own and placing it beside your laptop. Position it towards the wall so that the light bounces onto your face, or try placing it off to the side, behind your computer. Play around with the options and see what works best for you. Good lighting will make a HUGE difference in that first-second impression.

Raise Your Camera to Eye Level

Congratulations, Spielberg. You're directing a Zoom interview! And you're going to want to make sure you capture the best angle. This is easy to do. Just make sure your camera is elevated to point directly into your eyes. No phones in your hands. No laptops in your lap. At all costs we want to avoid the "I'm a serial killer looming over you" angle.

To get the right height, place your device on a stack of books about one arm's length away from your face. Once you're set up, feel free to tilt the screen down to make sure it's aligned with your eyes. If you're using a cell phone, the same rule applies! Prop the phone up on a stack of books and make sure the camera is eye level.

Watch Your Angles

Check Your Background

> "You'd be amazed at what I've seen in the background of some candidates' Zoom screens: A bong, dirty underwear, a filthy room, shirtless friends playing Xbox, confederate flags, and more. Pay attention to what we can see! All you have to do is turn your computer towards a blank wall and you'd be much better off!"
>
> —Very distracted Zoom interviewer

Let's keep this simple. *Everything* in the camera's eye matters. We've already talked about unconscious bias around apparel. Imagine the studies they'll do on one-second impressions of Zoom backgrounds.

Turn on your camera and see what it captures. Make sure there are minimal objects in the frame. Clean and declutter the entire area. Plants are good! If your bed is in the shot, make sure it's neatly made.

Sit Up Straight

> "I almost lost it when the applicant's screen came on and I realized she was lying in bed. Not sitting up in bed, which might have been forgiven, but lying down on a pillow, under a blanket! I asked her about it and she told me she was cold."
>
> —Employer warmed by their growing level of frustration

Posture matters. An upright spine conveys professionalism and attentiveness. Slouching conveys so many negative attributes they aren't worth listing. Your butt should touch the back of your chair. If you're doing it right, there will be a curve in your back. For most people this isn't their natural sitting position, so try putting a pillow behind your back as a tactile reminder to stay upright.

Smile When You Join the Call

> *"As a recruiter, I am constantly warning my clients to pay attention to the 'bookends' of their Zoom meetings. The beginning and ending seconds of a meeting make a huge difference. I've had somebody blow a perfect interview because in the last seconds, when the other person had said goodbye and turned off their video (but not logged out), the candidate dropped their guard, rolled their eyes, and muttered to themselves, 'What a f-ing jerk,' before closing the meeting. All it takes is one little thing."*
>
> *—Recruiter begging you not to blow it*

Our earlier chapter on in-person interviews covered the importance of smiling a *real* smile. One that gets your eyes in on the action. Make sure you're smiling before you enter the video meeting so it's the first thing the people on the other end will see. (And if you're the first one there, keep on smiling to make sure that's the first impression you give when they join.)

Smiling projects confidence and puts everyone at ease.

Show the Interviewer You're into It

Just like an in-person interview, you're going to start with the magical first sentence discussed earlier in this chapter. You'll use that sentence to start any interview regardless of format: in-person, over the phone, or over video.

However, being on camera can make it harder to convey enthusiasm. I recommend having a pad and pen ready, and let them see you writing things down. Not only does it show you're listening closely, but it creates an organic mechanism for you to give the two-second pause while you "read over your notes."

Embrace the Unexpected

> *"A mother of two young boys was interviewing with me over Zoom, and in spite of her putting them in front of a video*

> *before we started, her sons kept walking in and interrupting our interview. I'm sure she was frustrated, but it never showed. Watching the patience she had, the calm she exhibited, and the creative ways she kept redirecting them, said more about her character and what kind of employee she would be than anything I could've asked her. I gave her the job."*
>
> —*Employer who had a clear picture*

There's an old saying; "How do you make God laugh? Make a plan!" I guarantee if you do enough video interviews, something is going to go wrong. There will be some unforeseen interruption that will have you wanting to pull your hair out after all your careful preparation.

So, if your cat walks butt-first across your laptop, your kids barge in saying they need to go potty, or your roommate starts serenading the apartment from the shower, just roll with it. Your challenge is to calmly explain what's happening, and wave it off like it's nothing.

Video interview bloopers are the *ultimate* opportunity to show rather than tell someone how you react to pressure. Just take a deep breath and relax. Unexpected events are one of the best things that can happen to you while on camera if you handle them correctly.

Summary

- ☐ Do your homework before the interview so you can shine when you're in it.
- ☐ You've got 20 seconds to make an impression and spark a connection.
- ☐ Utilize the "magical first sentence" to kick off a great conversation.
- ☐ Make it a two-way conversation; tell stories and make them feel like *they're* doing well.
- ☐ Be ready to answer common interview questions and *always* ask your own.

11

How to Follow Up After the Interview

> *"I'd just finished interviewing with a company for a job I really wanted. I decided to be proactive and immediately sent a thank-you text to my interviewer. While I thought I wrote 'I can hardly contain my excitement about the possibility of working with your organization,' auto-correct changed 'excitement' to 'excrement.' Still got the job!"*
>
> —Job seeker currently retrieving their phone from the river they threw it in

Only 43% of candidates send their interviewer a thank-you note after an interview, according to a CareerBuilder survey.[1] This is a layup opportunity for candidates who want to stand out. Remember that most job opportunities have three to five final candidates. Your goal is to win this competition, which means you want to make sure you are memorable to every person in the process.

There are three techniques to writing a follow-up thank-you message, but all of them follow the overriding golden rule: talk about the interviewer—not yourself!

HOW TO FOLLOW UP AFTER THE INTERVIEW

Tell Them They've Increased Your Enthusiasm

There is no better way to compliment your interviewer than to say meeting them increased your interest in the role. Confirm what they suspected—that they were great in the interview!

> "When I walked in the door, I was already interested in the role, but talking to you cemented it for me. I am even more excited about the prospect of joining your team now."

Show You Listened to Them

Repeat something you learned or a key takeaway you had from speaking with them. Limit yourself to one or two examples, and share how their words affected you.

"I was pleasantly surprised to learn that 1% of company profits are donated to charity. That reinforced so many things for me about what's great about your company!"

Highlight Their Best Moment

"The candidates who send thank-you notes earn extra points in my book. It's polite and it makes them stand out. I'm not just looking for people with the right professional skills. I'm looking for people who know how to act like adults. I don't know when it happened, but it feels like civility and manners are a lost art."

—Employer who knows chivalry is dead

Revisiting their best moment from the interview falls in the category of "acceptable flattery." You do this by either (a) rehashing the best question they asked or (b) revisiting a moment they changed your mind or (c) describing a moment they taught you something. Keep this section brief, but end with a question to invite further post-interview dialogue.

"On the drive home from the interview, I kept replaying our debate about the right time to upsell a customer. After reflecting, you've changed my mind. I am swayed by the framing that you're not upselling—you're introducing them to everything the product can do. Who taught you to think about it this way? If it was a book I'd like to read it! Please let me know."

By expanding on that moment, you are highlighting what it would be like to work with you. In a nutshell, one great moment with you will lead to many more!

Summary

- [ ] Follow up with a thank-you note that focuses on the interviewer and invites more dialogue.

Go Get That Job!

12 You Must Negotiate

"There are only two situations in life where you can make $10,000 in 10 minutes simply by asking for it. One of them is when you're robbing a bank. The other is when you're negotiating a job offer. I know you hate negotiating because everybody is getting along and being nice, and you don't want to rock the boat. But trust me and be the bad guy for just a few minutes. It's the fastest $10,000 you'll ever make in your life without risking going to jail."

—Recruiter who has definitely considered robbing a bank

Your Brain Is Stupid

Congratulations! You now have an offer in hand. Big decision time. How much are you willing to pay to avoid having a single conversation about salary before you start?

    a. $5,000?
    b. $7,500?
    c. $15,000?
    d. $20,000?

Does that seem like a silly question? Do the numbers in options A through D seem ludicrous?

Well, they're not. In a 2019 survey of more than 50,000 job seekers on ZipRecruiter, 64% reported accepting the first offer they received, which means they chose one of the preceding answers.

The median salary in America is $56,000, and the average person holds a job for four years.[1] Negotiating for just 5% more during the initial offer is an additional $2,800 per year. That's almost $11,000 more over the lifetime of the job and that's without assuming you get annual raises![2]

I get it. For most people, negotiating is painful. It's not your fault. It's how your brain is wired. We all suffer from what's known in behavioral economics as the "endowment effect." In simple terms, our brains ascribe heightened value to something once it becomes ours. Within minutes of owning something, we embed it into our sense of self, and the idea of losing it becomes a threat to our identity. In other words, you're so afraid of losing that job offer, you've gone into fight or flight mode. To your muddled brain, negotiating might cause the employer to rescind the offer.

Let me reassure you that your brain is *stupid*. Employers *do not* rescind job offers because you ask for more. (They only rescind job offers if you're being an ass about it.) And oh, by the way, did I mention that employers who give you an offer are *also* affected by the endowment effect! They have stupid brains just like you do. Once they've made an offer they are as afraid of losing you as you are of losing them. Internalize this! Negotiating will not scare them away.

> *"I was hired onto the HR team several years ago. I accepted the $50,000 offer they gave me, and I was really excited because it was $10,000 more than I was making at my old job. My role was expanded this year and I got access to the HR files of all the employees at the company. Turns out I'm the lowest-paid person on the HR team by $15,000. I haven't been treated unfairly. I just started at a lower base. It burns me up inside because there is no redo button for the last five years."*
>
> —Employee rethinking every decision they've ever made

You Get What You Negotiate

When it comes to negotiating, Americans don't have many opportunities to practice. In our world, products and services are neatly labeled with bar codes and set prices.

You might think that jobs work the same way. And some jobs do. For example, there are rigid pay scales in the military that depend on rank. Likewise in government jobs where salaries are set by law or regulation. Even in the private sector, there are some jobs where you may not have room to maneuver like, say, if the industry is unionized or wages are paid hourly.

But the fact is that pay in *most* salaried jobs is set by negotiation. And that makes sense, once you think about it. In most companies, especially at the corporate level, there are no two people in the exact same job. That means there are no set pay scales—just ranges.

You have leeway. Let's make the most of it.

Negotiation Is Expected, and Priced into the First Offer

> *"I'm stunned by the number of people who accept the first offer. I'm tempted to be their career coach and say, 'That's really nice of you to accept so quickly, but actually, we're willing to pay you more.' Of course, I don't because that's not my job. It's one of the areas of life where nice guys finish last."*
>
> *—HR manager who really wants to coach you*

About one-third of all job candidates attempt to negotiate a job offer. Employers know this, but don't know which third of candidates will be the ones to try. As a result, they discount first offers by around 5% to 15% for ALL candidates. It's a rational strategy. So if you want to get paid what the employer really thinks you're worth, you have to negotiate. But what is the right number to ask for?

This information is really, really, really easy to find. Just go to www .ziprecruiter.com/Salaries. Enter the job title you've been offered and you'll immediately see the range of what real companies in your geographic region are paying for the same role. Spending five minutes doing this research will equip you with the data (and hopefully the confidence) to make at least one counteroffer without worrying about seeming unreasonable.

They Can't Guess What You Want

> *"Before I back down in a salary negotiation and accept the employer's offer, I submit my 'pity list.' It's the list of things that I care about that they probably don't, for which I say, 'Well, if I'm going to accept this offer that's lower than I think I deserve, the least you could do is give me a few extra vacation days, or a work from home day,' or whatever else I think they're willing to give on to finalize the deal."*
>
> *—Employee who loves making lists*

Before you enter a negotiation, you should ask yourself: What do I actually want?

It might seem obvious, in this context: You want a job, you want money, and you need a place to make free photocopies.

But there are other things that are important, too.

You may be looking for a flexible work schedule so you can balance work and family life. Maybe it's more vacation time if travel is important to you, or moving expenses if you are relocating for the new position. It could be a business card with a title that includes the word "Senior," or a great parking spot, or the ability to bring your dog to work.

All of that is negotiable. But some of those "wants" are more important than others.

Before any negotiation, make a list of your priorities, from top to bottom. If you can't get everything you want in a negotiation, the trick is to trade something at the bottom of the list for something really important at the top.

DON'T NEGOTIATE AGAINST YOURSELF

Don't Negotiate Against Yourself

You know what's worse than not negotiating? Negotiating against yourself!

Here are some practical tips for avoiding the most common negotiating mistakes inexperienced job seekers make while asking for more compensation.

Tell Employers You're Interviewing Multiple Places

Do you know the most effective tactic for inducing employers to increase an initial offer? Get multiple offers! The more jobs you apply to, the better chance you have at starting a competition for your services. Even if you have a "favorite," don't let that stop you from continuing to interview as many places as possible.

And here's the thing: you don't need to have multiple offers to trigger auction effects. Just telling employers you're interviewing at other companies is incredibly powerful. The more they like you, the faster they'll try to lock you down, and that includes meeting the price you name. Speaking of naming your price . . .

Anchor Higher

"My father told me, 'When you name your price, you should feel nauseous. If you don't feel nauseous, then you're not asking for enough.'"

—Employee whose dad wants to make them sick

Contrary to conventional wisdom, there is great benefit in giving the first number in a negotiation and more importantly, going *above* whatever it is you really want. This is what's known as an "anchor"—the number to which all others refer. Anchoring is a cognitive bias in which we unconsciously rely too heavily on the first piece of information we receive, and it clouds all future judgments. Retailers exploit this bias all the time. That's why you see the "original price" crossed out on a price tag, above where the "sale price" is displayed. (There is no such thing as an original price. All prices are made up.)

The same is true of employers. If you are looking to make $75,000 in a new job, ask for $95,000. Psychologically, $95,000 will become the anchor. If the hiring manager negotiates you down to $80,000, they will feel like they negotiated successfully and got a candidate worth $95,000 for less. The higher the anchor you set, the more room there is for both of you to win.

If the employer gives a number first, just remember how the psychology of anchoring works. Don't get dragged down by their anchor! If they go low, politely give a number back immediately, to re-anchor the negotiation higher. At a minimum you're creating a range.

Don't Automatically Accept the First Offer

The majority of job seekers we've interviewed have told us that when they did negotiate, they were able to increase the starting offer by at least 10%.

You don't have to accept the first number an employer throws out. You can always ask for more. Do it. That ten-minute conversation could be worth more than $10,000 a year.

Summary

- [ ] You must negotiate! Don't let the "endowment effect," or fear of losing the opportunity, stop you.
- [ ] Employers expect you to negotiate, and build that expectation into their initial offers.
- [ ] You can negotiate many things besides money, such as vacation, your schedule, and more.
- [ ] If you have multiple offers, employers will often feel pressure to hire you before someone else does and to sweeten the offer.
- [ ] "Anchor" by asking for a higher salary than you need so when you negotiate, you are starting from a higher number.
- [ ] Don't automatically accept the first offer. If you ask for more, you just might get it.

13

Negotiating Your Job Offer—A Step-by-Step Guide

No employer rescinds an offer because you make a counteroffer. It's only if you come off like an unappreciative entitled jerk that things can go south. But don't worry—I got you! Here's a step-by-step guide to make sure the negotiation goes smoothly.

Step 1: Celebrate with the Employer as Soon as You Get the Offer

Most job offers are delivered over the phone, but I don't care if they deliver it by email, text, TikTok, or singing telegram—however the employer reaches out to you, you will *immediately* tell them how excited you are to receive the offer. It should sound something like this:

> "I am excited to get this offer. Your company is my first choice! I can't wait to start working with you. Let me just look over the letter and I'll get back to you quickly."

This is you burying the hook. You just about accepted, which in their minds shifts you to "on the team." Hello endowment effect! Your value just became higher, as they now perceive you as theirs.

Step 2: Make a Smooth Counteroffer ———

Making a counteroffer is *so* much easier if you plan what to say ahead of time. If you only remember one thing about negotiating, remember this: you never have to give an ultimatum to get results. Here are three great negotiating tactics to choose from.

The Name-Your-Price Approach

You know what employers want in any negotiation? Certainty! That's why the time-tested best practice for making a counteroffer is to simply name a specific price at which the deal is done. This is the "vanilla" of negotiating techniques. Every employer has had it before, and using it will ruffle no feathers.

Here is the short version of the name-your-price approach in action:

"If you can do (x), we have a deal."

However, remember, the goal is to give the employer psychological certainty. They are afraid of losing you so you want to reiterate they have full control over making you say yes. I would name my price like this:

"This job is my first choice! I can already see myself working there. I want to say yes, but the offer came below what I needed. If you can do (x), we have a deal right now."

Important note: You want (x) to be at least 10% higher than what would actually make you happy. It's common for employers to counter below your new ask.

> ## Negotiating Tip: Use Monthly Rather Than Annual Dollars in Your Counter
>
> If you are uncomfortable asking for thousands of dollars more than they offered, try framing the counter in terms of a monthly amount versus annual. This has the added advantage of making it easier for you to explain your ask. "I need more salary to cover my monthly expenses."

> *If you can do $400 more per month, we have a deal.*
> Did that feel better? Congratulations—you just asked for $4,800 more per year. That's almost $20,000 during the four years you're likely to hold the job. Not bad for one conversation.

The One-Small-Problem Approach

If you just can't bring yourself to make a direct ask, I offer you the one-small-problem approach. This approach avoids what makes most people uncomfortable about negotiating: fearing their ask will be viewed as an ultimatum.

With this approach you serve up a problem that's yours and give the employer a chance to jump in and help you solve it. The technique is simple. After spending a day with the offer in-hand, reach back out to the employer and say the following:

"This company is definitely my first choice, and I'm determined to make it work. I have **one small problem** I need to solve before I can accept . . . (fill-in-the-blank reason)."

You can of course put many different endings on this statement:

"I have one small problem I need to solve before I can accept. Child-care is proving more expensive than I expected as I go back to work."

"I have one small problem I need to solve before I can accept. My student loan interest rates jump in December if I don't pay them down faster."

"I have one small problem I need to solve before I can accept. I've got a vacation prepaid for December and realize I won't have enough accrued time off from when I start to take it."

"I have one small problem I need to solve before I can accept. My spouse is worried about how much time I'll spend driving and the cost of commuting."

Whether it's more salary, more vacation time, a signing bonus, or a flexible work schedule, all options are on the table with this tactic. They already love you. Let them help you.

The Multiple-Offers Approach

MULTIPLE OFFERS MAKE NEGOTIATING EASY

"As an in-house recruiter, I can say that the thing that drives our team leaders crazy is hearing that a candidate is choosing between two offers. No one wants to lose their first choice, especially when their first choice is obviously in such high demand. They always ask me what I think we should do to close, and my answer is always the same. Money talks and bulls**t walks. Offer the candidate more money before they ask for it, and do it fast. You want to bump your offer to demonstrate your enthusiasm. It's much more effective than trying to counter after they've first had a higher offer from the competition. Nothing else speeds up a negotiation and favors the candidate like getting a second offer."

—*Recruiter who is not gonna lose this candidate*

Ready to bring a gun to this knife fight? There is one tactic that trumps them all. A technique so profound that it eliminates the need for any training I might give you and leaves the employer countering himself. The four most powerful words in a job seeker's repertoire are, "I have another offer."

It's really that simple. Getting more than one offer changes everything. Now you're entering the world of auctions where crazy things can happen. (Scientists call it "auction fever" when two or more competing parties overbid their predetermined limits in a frenzied desire to win.[1])

If you really dislike negotiating, then push yourself to get as many interviews going as possible. With two offers in hand, your endowment effect is mitigated. The employer's endowment effect is *maximized*. Now you get to relax and enjoy the journey. With three offers in hand you've entered what behavioral economists refer to as the "mojo zone" where your swagger becomes a palpable force that can physically impact the world. Okay, I just made that up, but that is how it feels to have three or more offers.

Once you get the offers, no need to do anything fancy. Just keep telling each side what the last offer is and let them decide when they want to drop out.

Step 3: Say Nothing Until They Do

> *"Everybody thinks the secret to negotiation is to say the right thing at the right time. The real secret to negotiation is to say nothing at the right time."*
>
> —*Employer who wouldn't tell me anything else*

Okay, you've made your counteroffer!

A common response from employers is to go quiet. It could be in your face-to-face conversation, over the phone, during a video chat, or a slow response to your email. In all cases my instructions to you remain the same. Whatever you do, after you've made an ask, zip it!

Don't. Say. Another. Word.

The silence that occurs after you pitch your counter may seem filled with portent and meaning, but I promise you it's not because they are recoiling from the audacity of your proposal. The silence is happening for only one reason—the employer is thinking about their response. Thinking about whether they can meet your ask. Thinking about whether to counter your counter. Thinking about what else they might say to entice you to accept their original offer.

If you try to "restart the conversation" or "end the awkwardness," you will end up negotiating against yourself. Even something innocuous like "I really want to be here" interrupts the employer's train of thought, which, until you spoke, was only focused on one thing—how to make you happy.

Fundamentally, if you start talking, they can't say yes. And just like that, you've spoiled your ask before you could hear an answer. Silence is golden. Use it to your advantage.

Step 4: Accept the Offer Correctly

After waiting out the silence, you get your reward when the employer informs you "we have a deal." Congratulations! However, remember that you still haven't signed an official offer letter or contract. Here are some tips to make sure the offer comes through as agreed.

Ask for It in Writing

Compensation is frequently negotiated verbally before a final offer is delivered. Now that you have the verbal agreement it's imperative to get it in writing. Your first order of business is to clarify *when* you can expect the written offer so that you can officially say yes. This is normally a formality, but don't let it linger. You don't want to be in a situation in which you and your new employer have a different recall of what was agreed to. *Especially* if you saved signing the paperwork until your agreed upon start date.

"I am so excited to take this job! Can I get the offer in writing today so I can officially say yes?"

Employer: "We will have you sign the formal offer letter the day you start along with all your other paperwork."

You: "No problem! Could I please have a copy of that offer letter now to review? Happy to formally sign it the first day I come in!"

Don't Sell Past the Close

> *"Nothing takes away the bad taste of difficult negotiations like a new employee excited to get to work."*
>
> —*Employer who is ready to move on*

As soon as you accept the offer, the only thing you'll talk about from this moment forward is the future.

"I can't wait to start on the 30th. It would be great if I could get a jump on coming up to speed. Do you have any recommendations for me?"

Don't rehash any of the negotiation points. Don't reiterate any contributions you think you can make. Don't talk about other offers you'll be turning down. This moment is about giving the employer certainty that you're excited, and you're definitely coming.

Pro Tip: Shift Immediately to "We"

With the shake of a hand or sending of an email, you've just become "the new person." Being the new person makes you an outsider. You want to lose that status and fully integrate as quickly as possible. A great hack for building camaraderie even before you start is to immediately use the words *we, us,* and *our,* instead of *me, I,* and *my.*

Inclusive language shows that you view yourself as "on the team" and that you measure team success as your success.

"I can't wait to start. We are going to make this product fly off the shelves!"

"What are our goals for the quarter?"

"You can count on us to get the production pipeline humming."

In most cases, it takes people months to use inclusive language after starting a new job. Try it to see how it transforms your onboarding experience.

Summary

☐ Negotiating is expected and will make them want you more.

☐ You don't ever have to give an ultimatum to get something out of a negotiation.

☐ Having multiple offers is like having superpowers.

☐ *Always* get the offer in writing.

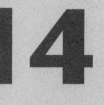

14

How to Quit Your Current Job the Right Way

It takes many good deeds to build a good reputation, and only one bad one to lose it.

—Benjamin Franklin

How you leave a job is *just as* important as how you come in. Quitting, no matter how artfully executed, is an act of rejection. Even though it's not malicious, it still feels bad for your employer and the colleagues you're leaving behind. Replacing you and covering the extra work your departure creates all fall into the category of "frustrating problems." By doing everything you can to soften the blow, you're making an investment in your future. Here are the things to remember to have a successful and amicable separation.

Don't Quit Your Job Until You Have an Offer Letter in Writing

"The same day I got a verbal job offer, I gave my two weeks' notice to my current employer. Hours later, the new employer called back and said they were sorry, but they were having trouble getting my salary level approved by HR. It took four

> *days to iron out, but when the offer letter came in, I was forced to take $5,000 less than we'd originally discussed. I felt like an idiot."*
>
> —Employee who had already spent that $5,000 in her mind

No matter how confident you are that you're off to greener pastures, do not speak to anyone at your current job until you have these three things: the offer letter, the offer letter, and lastly, the offer letter.

It's great that you've talked to the hiring manager at your new potential place of employment and come to a verbal agreement, but until you have the offer letter in writing, the deal isn't done. It's unlikely, but things *can* happen: the department you're joining could get eliminated. The CEO's nephew could need a job. The company could go into a hiring freeze. Don't take an unnecessary risk by resigning until you have somewhere to go—in writing. There are few things worse for your relationship with a current employer than trying to recant a resignation.

Always Notify Your Direct Manager First—Don't Skip Levels

There is a saying you'll hear if you ever get the opportunity to participate in management training: "People don't leave companies, they leave managers." Fair or not, your departure will reflect on your boss. They'll be judged for not knowing you were unhappy, or recognizing you were undercompensated, or for being unable to convince you to stay. When bad things happen, it creates vivid memories. Today is a very bad day for them. They will remember everything about how you resign.

Hopefully you have a good relationship with your manager and you'll be parting with the company on good terms. Even if you aren't, it's in your best interest to show respect to the person you have been working for. That person's life is about to get harder without the work you do, so consider it your final task to make that transition as easy as possible. This will be the lasting impression you leave, and the one your manager will recall should you need a favor or recommendation from them in the future.

When you resign, here's how to do it well:

- Tell your manager you're putting in your resignation and give at least two weeks, notice.
- Explain why you accepted the new job (versus focusing on why you were looking).
- Ask for input on how to communicate that you're leaving to the rest of the team. Be clear on the plan and follow it. Don't let rumors of your departure get ahead of your manager. The more your manager feels out of control, the worse the situation is for him or her.
- Offer to assist in hiring a replacement for yourself including writing the job description, vetting candidates, and conducting interviews.
- Have a written list of what you're currently responsible for and suggestions for whom to offload those to.
- Offer to train someone internally if there isn't a ready-to-go handoff candidate for something you do.

Collaborating this way makes you and your manager owners/partners of transitioning you out gracefully. It will make a big difference in your long-term relationship.

No Touchdown Dances

While the new job is good news for you, it is bad news for everyone left on the team. They'll need to find someone to replace you, someone to cover your responsibilities, someone to onboard and train your replacement, and finally deal with the reality that the familiar is about to be replaced with the unknown. It sucks and they aren't happy. Be mindful of their state.

Don't overdo your excitement about the new job. Don't brag about your new salary. And whatever you do, don't rehash things you don't like about your current job. Here are the sentences to embrace:

- "I'm going to miss you."
- "Working with you was one of my favorite parts of this job."
- "I learned a lot from you."
- "The hardest part about leaving is how much I enjoyed working with all of you."
- "I hope we get to work together again."

Any impulse you have to celebrate should be focused on the team—not your future. Help them find closure by celebrating your time together. Don't let the last thing they remember be you strutting out the door.

What to Do If They Counter

Remember the endowment effect we talked about earlier? Congratulations, on a scale from one to ten, you just sent it to an 11. There is *nothing* that will make your current company appreciate your value more than telling them you plan to leave. This can create the dynamic in which you've accepted a new offer, but the bidding has just begun.

A Lot of Employers Will Offer a Counter

Brace yourself. There's a good chance you're going to be asked some variation of, "What would it take to get you to stay?"

Never answer this question in the first meeting. The right response is "Let me give it real thought and get back to you tomorrow." You want the full organization to have time to reflect on what your departure means. This will make the previously impossible, suddenly become possible—more money, a new title, more vacation time, changes to reporting structure, or even all of the above. Ask and ye shall likely receive.

But before making any ask, be sure there is a scenario in which you'd be willing to actually stay. Remember, the people from your former jobs are the ones most likely to get you your next one. Do not burn bridges here by negotiating in bad faith.

If You're Willing to Stay, Make Your Ask *Big*

If you are willing to stay, the key to this moment is going *big*. You have nothing to lose with another offer in hand, so you might as well ask for everything and discover the limits. Right now your "cost" has nothing to do with what the company pays you and everything to do with the full price tag of replacing you. Here is my advice for making the most of this moment:

- Ask for *a minimum* of 5% more than your *new* offer.
- Design the job you want—hours, work from home flexibility, and weekend/vacation boundaries.

- Demand opportunities to keep learning—areas of responsibility, conferences, or subsidization of ongoing education.
- Remove toxic people—eliminate anything you do that requires you to interact with people you don't like.
- Optimize your workspace—ask for an office, preferred cubicle location, or budget to improve your environment.
- Give a time limit of 24 hours. Don't let them haggle with you while your two weeks' notice is running out.

This isn't an exhaustive list of considerations, but it captures the essence of what I'm telling you. *Nothing* is off the table. Make your ask grandiose. The worst they can do is say no.

If You Accept the Counter, Tell the Other Company Immediately

You made your big ask and, whoa, they gave it to you. This is a moment to follow all the best practices outlined in Chapter 12, "You Must Negotiate." Celebrate with them immediately and make sure they give it to you in writing!

Once you have it in writing, you have one final uncomfortable task to complete: notifying the company whose offer you accepted that you're pulling out. Here's how to do it well:

- **Be quick.** The longer you wait, the more you risk creating ill will.
- **Be honest.** Tell the company exactly why you're reneging. Learning that your current company valued you highly will only make the new company like you more.
- **Be prepared.** Don't be surprised if the new company tries to increase their offer. This is exactly the kind of situation in which an auction frenzy can occur. You'll need to decide how comfortable you are letting the two sides continue to bid up.

Don't Be Surprised If You Remain Unhappy After Accepting a Counteroffer

The problem with achieving your goals is the person you had to become to reach those goals has different goals.

—Mark Cuban

The reality is it's difficult for any of us to describe what will make us happy. It's easy to think in the abstract that more money, authority, or appreciation would make the difference, but the reality is that ambitious people are rarely satisfied.

Can you really be happy if you stay? The data says even odds the answer is no. Of the employees who accept a counteroffer, 50% end up leaving within a year.[1] Don't beat yourself up if you find yourself back on the market shortly after getting everything you thought you wanted. The good news is that after reading this book, you're a job-seeking expert, so the next job will be easier to get!

Summary

☐ Make sure you have your new job offer in writing before you quit your current one.

☐ Always tell your direct manager about your resignation first and work with them on a transition plan.

☐ Don't act overly excited about leaving your current job. Be careful to maintain old work relationships.

☐ If your current company wants to provide a counteroffer, make sure the compensation and other benefits of staying are big.

☐ If you accept a counteroffer from your current employer, let the other company know immediately.

☐ Keep in mind that accepting a counteroffer won't necessarily make you happier.

15 Congratulations on the New Job! Let Me Know How It Went!

If you've followed all my advice, then it's only a matter of time before you're ready for this, the final chapter in the book. The advice here is simple.

Celebrate!

You worked your butt off (although not as hard as you would have had to have worked before reading this book), you got the job, so make sure you celebrate your win.

And since everybody loves a good party, myself included, would you mind inviting me to join your celebration? There is nothing that gets me and the ZipRecruiter team more fired up than helping people find work. So please message me and share your job search story, both the good and the bad, the ups and the downs. Let me know if this book helped you find your first job, get a better job, change careers, or get back into the workforce.

Let me know about your job search by sending me a message at this page www.ziprecruiter.com/gethirednow

Congratulations on your success!

—Ian Siegel

Appendix: Before You Start the Search

> *"I tell the people I work with that the best time to be looking for a job is while you still have one and before you need one. Obviously, that doesn't always happen, so regardless of their situation, the advice I have for them is that there's always a positive angle to take on whatever situation they're in. Lead with the positive."*
>
> —Recruiter and ray of sunshine

I'm eager to make job search easy for you, but before we dive in, you might be in a situation that requires you to take action right away. You only need to read this appendix if any of the following situations apply to you:

- You were laid off or fired.
- You are about to graduate from school.
- You are coming out of the military.
- You are returning to the workforce after a gap in your work history.

If you DO fall into one of those categories, read on so we can make sure you knock out the paperwork, leverage the programs, or explore the resources that won't be available to you later on if you miss the window. Once you're done, head on back to Chapter 1 where the real work begins!

You Were Laid Off or Fired

Sorry to hear it. But you're not alone. In 2020 more than 20 million people went through the same thing.[1] In our annual job seeker surveys, job loss tends to be the second most common reason someone is looking for a job. (#1 is "looking for a better job.")

Losing a job can be painful. But don't let that stop you from leaving in a way that sets you up for success. Here is the list of things to do immediately.

Check for Accrued Unpaid Vacation Days, Sick Days, or Overtime

Request to be paid out for any accrued vacation days that you did not use. Likewise with sick days and overtime. Many states mandate that employers pay employees for unused vacation days, so the law is likely on your side. Accrued vacation days are often noted on your paycheck, or you can put in a request with the HR department for that information.

Don't Forget the Paperwork: COBRA and Your 401(k)

The US government has a program called the Consolidated Omnibus Budget Reconciliation Act—COBRA, for short. It provides health insurance coverage for those who lose their health insurance when they lose their jobs. Here's the catch: your old employer has to fill out the paperwork for you to be eligible. Don't walk out the door until you are sure that your former boss is taking care of it.

Likewise with any 401(k) accounts. That's your money, and you should make sure to roll it over to an investment account you control. Complete this as soon as you can.

Check for Severance Pay

If you have been let go, don't go without asking your employer about severance pay, especially if you were let go in a layoff rather than terminated for cause. In a few states, there are government-mandated severance requirements for employers if the number of people let go exceeds a threshold. You might receive months' worth of salary and/or health insurance coverage, depending on your employer.

And even if a severance package isn't mandated in your case, it usually pays to ask. Employers are often concerned about ex-employees coming back and suing them for some reason, so they usually ask you to sign a legal document agreeing not to sue them in the future, and to incentivize you to sign it, they typically give a severance package once you do. If you have reason to think you might want to take legal action in the future, consult with a lawyer, but if you don't think it's in the realm of possibility, consider signing it if they offer you a severance package that meets with your approval.

> *"I worked for a fulfillment center, and was laid off with a bunch of my co-workers with only one week of severance. They asked me to sign some sort of document agreeing never to sue them for anything in the future. I was a bit insulted by the one week of severance, so I told them there was no reason for me to sign that thing just out of the kindness of my heart. Now I'm not the type of guy who would ever sue my ex-employer for anything anyway, but I guess they didn't realize that, because they came back and gave me two months of severance in exchange for signing, which I happily accepted. I feel bad for the guys that just signed it for no reason at all though."*
> —*Employee who was able to breathe a little easier*

Send a Classy Goodbye Email

Your first order of business is to write an email to everybody you know at the company you're leaving. The purpose of the email is to say what a great experience you've had, give a general idea of what type of opportunities you're looking for next, and make it easy for people to keep in touch with you.

To be clear, this is a time for professionalism. Regardless of whether the breakup was amicable or awful, your email should be 100% positive. Here's some language you could use:

Dear friends,

I'm writing with the sad news that I will be leaving the company. I have worked at Left Foot Shoes for over three years, and I have enjoyed every minute of it. I've loved working with each and every one of you, and am so grateful for the relationships we have built, and hopefully, will continue to build. I'm excited by all the opportunities that lie ahead of me, and plan to continue my career in accounting. I hope you'll keep in touch with me. My personal email is xxx@gmail.com.

You should also take the time to immediately request a LinkedIn connection with everybody you know at your company. And don't just connect with the people you were close with, but everybody you *ever* knew at the company. Later in the book we'll talk about how powerful your network can be in your job search. Even acquaintances make a difference.

> *"I was so embarrassed about getting fired that I tried to leave the company as fast as I could without really saying goodbye to any of my friends or colleagues. At the last minute though, I wrote a very short email thanking everybody for a great four years and included my personal email address. I can't tell you how lucky I was that I did that. That night, aside from all the wonderful emails I got from my coworkers telling me how much they enjoyed working with me, one person pointed me to a new job opportunity. Three weeks later, I was hired!"*
> —Employee who turned it around with one email

Apply for Unemployment Benefits

Every month you were working, a portion of your paycheck went to unemployment insurance. Your employer had to pay in, too. There's no shame in claiming what is rightfully yours. This program is specifically designed for a person in your situation. Use it. The Department of Labor's website can help you find information about filing for unemployment in your state: www.dol.gov/general/topic/unemployment-insurance.

> *"I was let go six months into my first job after college. My dad told me to file for unemployment, but I didn't want to be one of those people supported by the government or take money away from those that really needed it. Then my dad sat me down, pulled out my last paycheck, and pointed to a line labeled 'UI Tax.' He said, 'That UI stands for unemployment insurance. It's not welfare. It's insurance that you bought with your own money so that if and when this day came, you would still have some income.' I realized he was right, and applied the next day."*
> —*Employee who still pays into UI each paycheck*

Own Your Bad News

The sooner you accept that your previous job is over, the easier it will be for you to find the next one. If you're laid off, change your LinkedIn profile the day it happens. And write a post like this on your social media accounts:

> "My five wonderful years at Company X unexpectedly came to an end today due to a mass layoff caused by the recession. I am grateful for the valuable experience and my amazing team, and I will miss all my fabulous colleagues. If anyone hears of an exciting opportunity in communications or public relations, please let me know!"

You're likely to get many likes and comments from your old colleagues, describing how much they enjoyed working with you and how much they will miss you. Those comments are social proof that you were well-liked in your old job when reviewed by new prospective employers.

They also tell the world you're looking for something. Networking your way to a new job is one of the most effective tactics for job seekers. Now you're not just looking for a job on your own. You have a community doing it with you.

Explore Training or Retraining

The job you just lost might never reappear. That's an increasingly common experience as technology changes the job market. You DO NOT need to go back to school for another degree.

There are plenty of short-term or online courses available that provide skills and certifications that can help you retool for a new job, perhaps in a new industry. You can develop proficiency for many in-demand skills in weeks, not months.

While many online courses from private course providers are free or cheap online, it's worth seeing what the government offers, too. Contact an American Job Center or call the Employment and Training Administration's (ETA) toll-free helpline at 1-877-US-2JOBS to find a list of training programs and job search services for laid-off workers that are available near you.

Start Searching for a Job Immediately

After losing your own job, you might feel tempted to withdraw from the working world for a while. And if you're collecting severance pay or expect to receive unemployment insurance for the next 26 weeks or so, you may feel that you can afford to wait.

But the people who have the best luck finding a new job tend to be those who start looking right away. It can often take longer than you expect to find a job you like, go through the interview process, get an offer, and sign on the dotted line. So think of unemployment benefits as a safety net, not a salary. And the shorter the gap in your work history, the easier it is to get re-hired. That's especially true if there are many people losing their jobs at once. Don't wait.

Treat the Job You Lost as an Asset

Your last job can provide you references, letters of recommendation, and portfolio pieces. You might feel bitter about being let go—but set that aside. You want to be on the best terms possible with your previous employer and colleagues. Don't just disappear. Stay in touch with people. Use your last job as your foot in the door to the next one.

> *"When my boss fired me, I was furious. After two years, with no warning, he said he couldn't afford to pay me anymore and that today would be my last day. I just about cursed him out, but fortunately I got control of myself and walked out the door to cool off. When I collected my last paycheck he gave me an*

incredible recommendation letter that I'm convinced is what closed the deal for me on my next job. Months later, I went back to tell him how close I was to blowing my stack when he fired me, and we had a good laugh, but I don't think he would've been laughing if I had lost control that day."
— *Employee who sure is glad he took that walk*

You Are About to Graduate from School

Make the Most of Your Student Status

If you're about to graduate from school, keep in mind that your power as a job seeker is about to become greatly diminished on graduation day, so you'll want to make the most of your "student status" while you still can. Students have a huge networking advantage over the general population and a unique way to set themselves apart. People generally want to go out of their way to help students of any age.

As a student it's much easier to network with employees at companies that interest you. Messages like, "I'm a graduating student from [insert school name] in June, and I'm fascinated by your industry. Would you be willing to spend 15 minutes on the phone answering some of my questions?" are going to work. Alumni make GREAT targets for outreach of this nature.

Use Your School's Free Resources

The other advantage you have while still a student is access to your school's career resources. Every school's are different, but even the least-developed school career center will give you a leg up on the competition. It's like having your own (free) personal assistant setting up opportunities for you in the form of job fairs, networking events, recruiting seminars, career counseling, and most importantly, job listings that are sometimes only made available to students.

> *"I wasn't that into college when I attended, but the alumni from my university go out of their way to help me. There's a real feeling of school spirit that I now appreciate. Those connections are helping me find work. I hope someday to be in a position where I can pay it forward."*
> —Employee who cheers harder for his school football team now

You Are Coming Out of the Military

First of all, thank you for your service. And congratulations—your experience will be something that sets you apart. About 11% of job seekers on ZipRecruiter are veterans and about 17% of job postings explicitly call on veterans to apply. The share of job postings listing "military experience" as a desired skill keeps rising.[2] Employers love hiring veterans.

Second, make sure to consider taking advantage of the Career Skills Programs, also known as SkillBridge. These unique programs let you work for a private-sector employer for up to six months before your separation or retirement. They're free for the employer and allow you to learn on the job while still earning your military salary. You can learn about the SkillBridge program at https://dodskillbridge.usalearning.gov.

Third, explore the Transition Assistance Program (TAP), developed by seven different government departments and agencies, including the Departments of Labor, Defense, and Education. There are people whose entire job is to make sure you have a job after you finish your service. Take advantage of their help. You can learn more about TAP workshops, courses, apprenticeships, and resources here: www.dol.gov/agencies/vets/programs/tap.

And finally, check out the tools from the Defense Department, Labor Department, and RAND Corporation that help you translate military courses and experience into in-demand civilian job skills. All those military training programs, on the job qualifications, special assignments, detachments and deployments you completed in uniform could mean real advantages in the job market. Some useful tools can be found here: www.military.com/veteran-jobs/skills-translator, www.careeronestop.org /BusinessCenter/Toolkit/civilian-to-military-translator.aspx, and www .rand.org/pubs/tools/TL160z2-2.html.

"I never served in the military, but my father and brother did. Resumes from people who have served go to the top of the pile when I'm hiring. I personally want to do whatever I can to help the people who have risked their lives to keep us safe. As far as I'm concerned, US military service is the best reference a candidate can have."
—Employer who is thankful for your service

You Are Returning to the Workforce After a Gap in Your Work History

There's that uncomfortable moment in many job interviews where an employer, looking through a resume, will ask: "So . . . what were you doing from 2008 to 2010?"

I need you to internalize a truth; gaps don't matter. You might have been raising a child, meditating in an ashram, or dealing with a recession that knocked out your industry. Lots of people have gaps. Don't hide them. The key will be telling the employer what you learned or how you've improved as a person due to the experience you had. Emphasize that you're ready to work now. The time off has made you more committed than ever. We'll cover more about how to handle a gap in your written resume later in the book.

"I was a full-time mom of four children for 20 years before I started looking for accounting work again. Who ended up hiring me? An accounting firm owner who was a mother of two herself. I think she realized if I could raise four kids, balancing books for customers would be a breeze. Mom power!"
—Employee and proud mom

Summary

I get it. Books are long. And not everything speaks directly to your situation. If you don't have the patience to read this whole book, or if you've read it and are just looking for a quick reference guide, here is a summary version.

Preface: Launch Points

People go into job searches in many different ways, and some of those require you to take action before reading this book.

I Was Laid Off or Fired

- **Make sure you get paid** for any accrued unpaid vacation days/sick days/overtime.
- **Sign up for COBRA** (health insurance).
- **Transfer 401(k) money out of the company's 401(k) plan.**
- Ask **about a severance package** to give yourself an extra financial cushion while looking for a job, and don't sign any legal agreements unless they offer compensation.
- **Send a classy goodbye email to all your co-workers.** Include your personal email address so they can stay in touch.
- **Send LinkedIn connection requests** to capture the value of the relationships you built.
- **Apply for unemployment benefits,** immediately. You've been paying for this insurance program in every paycheck. Use it.
- **Own your bad news** by posting it to your social media accounts, in a positive fashion, to let your network know you're looking for work.
- **Consider training** as a supplement to your job search.

- **Start your job search immediately**. People who look for work right after losing a job have more success in finding a new job.
- **Keep in touch with the people from your former job**. Your network is a huge asset in a job search.

I Am About to Graduate from School

If you're about to graduate from school, you'll want to jump into the search as aggressively as possible to **make the most of your "student status" while you still can**. That includes using your networking advantage by soliciting alumni as a student, and **using all your school's free career center resources**, which are sometimes quite valuable.

I Am Coming Out of the Military

Thank you for your service! Employers love hiring veterans, so take advantage of that and **use all the military resources at your disposal**, including the Career Skills Programs (SkillBridge), and the Transition Assistance Program (TAP). Also make sure you check out all the available tools from the Defense Department, Labor Department, and RAND Corporation that help you translate military experience into in-demand civilian job skills.

I Am Returning to the Workforce After a Gap in My Work History

Gaps don't matter. Lots of people have gaps, so don't be defensive about them. Be truthful about them and focus on the positive aspects of your time away from the workforce.

I Am Currently Employed but Looking for a New Job

The best time to get a new job is while you're still in your old one. It's a positive signal to new employers that will make your search significantly easier.

Introduction: Nobody Teaches You How to Be a Job Seeker

Much of the conventional wisdom about the job search process is wrong since job search moved online. Here's a walk-through of how things work today.

Part One: Get Prepared Now!

Chapter 1: Accept the Truth About Bias

Everybody has bias, including you. Every person you meet during the hiring process is ruled by bias they can't control. Our goal is not to eliminate peoples' biases, but rather, to **use awareness of bias to do better at every point of the job search process**. Understanding how bias works is as important as writing an effective resume.

Chapter 2: Write a Resume That Works

Get Past the Robots

Most resumes are read by a robot before they are read by a human. **The sole purpose of your resume is to get past the robots** and into human hands. There are many things you can do to improve your chances.

- **Use the simplest resume template you can find** so the robots won't have any problem parsing it.
- **Use generic job titles** for your past experience, because you want the robots to match the job titles that employers use in their job postings.
- **Write like a caveman**, meaning use simple language so that the robots can clearly decipher your skills and experience. Many times your resume is turned into a brief summary for humans, so simple language helps there as well.
- **Use numbers** to describe your career accomplishments and impact in a concrete way. This will make summarization of your accomplishments cleaner.

- **List your job skills.** Put them in their own section. Be explicit in describing them, especially since employers are now prioritizing specific, demonstrable skills. When listing these skills, be precise in what they are and the number of years you've practiced them.
- **Include all licenses and certifications.** If you have a license, include the license number.

Coming Out of School with No Prior Work Experience

If you're looking for your first job after school:

- **List any work experience you have**, in addition to listing school experiences like academics, jobs, internships, extracurricular activities, community service, or any other productive way you've spent your time.
- **Put your Education section at the top**, with your school name, your full GPA or your major GPA (if that's higher). If both your GPAs were poor, don't worry. No one in the real world will ever bring up your GPA if you don't.
- Remember that **employers consider soft skills essential.** Anything you can do to show these off works in your favor.

Be Honest About Gaps in Your Work Experience

Don't leave gaps in your resume blank. Be honest about gaps in your work experience, because there's always a way to turn those gaps into assets for your job search.

- **If you've been laid off**, include the job experience on your resume, and then add a bullet point about the reason why you were laid off.
- **If you were fired**, you should still include the job experience, but it's best *not* to note that you were fired on your resume and just discuss it during your interview.
- **If you were raising children**, list that as your experience, and make the details as engaging as possible about what you accomplished.
- **If you spent time figuring out what you really wanted to do**, list that on your resume but be specific and focus on the things you did that encouraged you to grow.

- **If you were incarcerated,** it's important to include that on your resume. List the institution, the years you were incarcerated, a general mention of the type of offense (without getting too specific), and be sure to include any positive things you did during your incarceration that reflect well on you and your character.
- **If you were caring for somebody sick** (possibly even yourself), briefly explain the matter in a general way, without providing too much information, especially about the person you cared for. Be prepared to talk about your time as a caregiver, and how you used your strengths during that time.

Check Your Resume for Grammar and Spelling

Using poor grammar and spelling on your resume is like speaking to somebody with lettuce in your teeth: people will be too distracted to pay attention to the important stuff you have to say. Double-check your spelling and grammar, and then have at least one friend review it again.

Get All the Little Resume Details Right

Make sure you're getting these parts of your resume right:

- Include your full legal name
- Phone number: Use your cell phone number or the number that you most reliably answer. You *must* be ready to answer this phone at all times while job hunting.
- Email address: If you are in college or graduate school, it is a good idea to use your official school email address. It shows employers that you really attend the school you say you do. If you are already in the workforce, use your personal email address, *not* your business email address. There is real bias over what email provider you use. Time to drop the @hotmail.com or @earthlink.net email address and upgrade to Outlook or Gmail.
- Physical address: Include your city, state, and zip code. If you're open to moving or explicitly looking to move, include "open to relocating" or "planning to relocate."

Should You Pay for a Resume-Writing Service?

Resume writing services are usually worth the money, especially since the people running them usually spend all day, every day, focused on something that you're only doing once every few years: writing a resume. Just make sure you do your homework and use a service that is competent and reputable.

Give Your Resume the Robot Test

When you're done with your resume, **upload it to ZipRecruiter to see if our robots parse it correctly**. If our robots can't read your resume, you can be sure that other systems are going to have even worse problems.

Chapter 3: Polish Your Online Brand

Before you start searching for jobs, you need to review, clean up, and possibly hide your social network content from prospective employers. **In one CareerBuilder survey, over 50% of employers reported passing on a candidate because of something they found on one of their social networks.**

How to Clean Up Your Social Media Accounts

The easiest way to clean up your social media accounts is simply to **make your accounts private**, because employers can't see what they can't find. If you are looking for the type of job where companies are going to expect to see your online presence, then you'll have to go **through each social media account individually** and decide which pictures, articles, and videos are those that will reflect well on you. Make sure you scroll all the way back to the beginning of your social media life in each account. **The one social media account you should *not* set to private is LinkedIn**, since that's how employers can find out more about you.

Get Your References Ready

One in three candidates is eliminated from consideration after a reference check, so **having good references is critical to landing a job. The best references by far are previous employers and co-workers**, but you may also want to use clients, customers, commanding officers in the military, or even teachers. Even references from your personal life, like a religious leader or another volunteer in a charitable organization you give your time to, can work in rare cases. You need to ask all potential references to **make sure they are going to say positive things about you.** Remember to **reconnect with each reference every time you give their contact information to a potential employer**, and make sure to tell them about the specifics of the job you're applying to.

Get Your Recommendation Letters in Place

A recommendation letter is a more concise, written version of a reference, but with one big advantage: with your reference's permission, you can write the letter yourself to custom-tailor it to deliver exactly the message you want. This doesn't mean to forge a letter, but rather, write the first draft for your reference for them to edit as they see fit. Start with a clear opening statement, include a description of the professional relationship between you, add concrete examples of what you did well, and finish with an unequivocal endorsement of your future potential.

Chapter 4: Network to Build Relationships

Networking Is an Awesome, Ridiculous, Unfair Advantage. Use It!

Somewhere between 60% and 85% of jobs are filled by networking. It's the most common reason an otherwise qualified candidate didn't get the job. Many job openings never get posted or announced because the hiring manager creates the role internally to bring in a specific known candidate. **The job search, and much of life, is about relationships, and those relationships are built upon a foundation of networking.**

How to Network

The average person knows 600 people. **You need to use that network of people to help you.** Interestingly, it is our weak connections to people (those people who you do not see on a regular basis), rather than the strong ones, that actually make a difference. **Your job is to build the biggest network of weak ties you can.**

- **Invite everyone you know (and don't know) to connect on social media**. The more people you're connected to, the more opportunities you create for yourself.

- **Smash that "like" button.** Don't be a lurker. Studies show that the more you "give" by liking things, the more people are willing to help you in return.
- **People on social media are primed to help you,** just don't make asking for help the first thing you do.
- **Words and tone matter,** so make sure your posts are positive and written to position you as somebody others would want to recommend.
- **Share openly about whatever it is that you're passionate about** to attract others like you.
- **People are attracted to momentum,** so put your introversion away and tell people how you're spending your time, particularly if it's about self-improving.
- **Post stories.** People love before and after stories. They can be about anything.
- **Avoid controversial topics** like politics, religion, population health, or conspiracy theories.

In the Real World, Don't Network for a Job, Network for a Relationship

The whole point of networking is to make a personal connection with somebody, and just about the least personal, most utilitarian question you could ask somebody is "What do you do?" Instead, **start with the personal stuff.**

Make the Most of a Formal Networking Meeting

When you do meet with somebody to ask for help or advice, plan ahead so you get a positive outcome. **Be explicit in what you're asking for,** stay humble in your discussions with them, and most importantly, try to find something you can help them with, even if it's as simple as just recommending a new restaurant.

Part Two: Find the Right Job!

Chapter 5: Use Job Sites That Have These Features

Job search technology has gone through a revolution in the past eight years, so make sure you use sites that have these features.

Feature 1: Has All the Jobs in One Place

Some job sites only display jobs employers pay to post, but **aggregators make *all* jobs from many sites searchable in one place.** The list of aggregators include ZipRecruiter, LinkedIn, Monster, and Indeed.

Feature 2: Enables You to Apply to Jobs with One Click

One of the most frustrating realities of job search is that many employers require job boards to send you offsite to the company's corporate job page in order to put in an application. **The best sites have a one-click apply feature** that allows you to submit an application to most jobs without ever leaving the job site interface. If you don't see a "one-click" or "one-tap" apply option on your current job site, switch to one of the big, modern job boards.

Feature 3: Picks Jobs Just For You

Thanks to the emergence of artificial intelligence (AI), you now live in a golden age where AI can pick "just right" jobs for you as soon as they are posted. Make sure you **use a job site that alerts you to a job match the moment the job goes live**. The speed with which you apply to a job is highly correlated with getting hired.

Feature 4: Shows You What the Robots See

All job sites use robots to try to extract who you are from your resume, but the average resume parser is only about 60% accurate in interpreting resumes. The best sites show you what your online resume looks like and let you correct and enrich the information in your profile.

Feature 5: Alerts You to a Job Match as Soon as the Job Goes Live

The absolute best time to apply to a job is one second after the recruiter posts it. More than 25% of jobs are filled with candidates who applied within the first two days, while 50% tend to be people who applied within the first week. Don't waste your time on sites that aren't giving you instant notifications of new job postings.

Feature 6: Enables Feedback on Individual Job Suggestions

Look for sites with the option to give a thumbs up or down, or maybe a happy/sad face rating, on a delivered suggestion. That feedback is sent back to the algorithm to infer your preferences around things like salary range, geography, and company size so that your recommendations keep increasing over time.

Feature 7: Shows You How Good a Match You Are for Every Job

The second most common complaint from job seekers after not getting a response to an application is not knowing which jobs to apply to. Job search companies can now use AI to show you how good a match you are for open jobs. Use sites that explicitly call out whether or not applying makes sense!

Feature 8: Keeps Track of Your Applications

Make sure to **use a service that keeps a record of the jobs you've applied to so you can easily find them again**. This is particularly important if the employer contacts you after you've applied. You want to be able to review the details of the position before speaking with them.

Feature 9: Lets You Know Your Application Status

The number-one complaint from job seekers around the world is applying to a job and not hearing anything back. Make sure the job site you're using tells you when the employer reads your resume, when they review it again, and when they give you a positive rating. **If you're not getting application status updates, find a site that provides them.**

Feature 10: Helps You Get Recruited

Getting recruited is a *way* better way to discover a new opportunity than actually trying to *find* one. Use a job site that presents you to employers like a recruiter would. **In the future of job search you don't apply to jobs. The employers apply to you.**

Chapter 6: Tools You *Have* to Use in Your Search

You Must Be on ZipRecruiter

ZipRecruiter is the number-one ranked job search app in the United States for four years running, and is at the forefront of technological innovation and market design to assist you in your job search. No other job site is doing all the things ZipRecruiter has already done.

You Must Be on LinkedIn

LinkedIn is the professional social network. **Everyone looking for a career versus just finding a job should be on LinkedIn.** Use LinkedIn to find the pages of companies you're interested in, invite people you know to connect, and find people you have a connection to.

On LinkedIn, you can expand your network by joining active professional groups, ask people to write you recommendations, send messages to connections, and see who is looking at your profile. To get even more value, you should periodically post things that catch your professional interest, and like/comment on others' posts. You can also use LinkedIn to learn more about the companies and the people at those companies you'll be meeting with for interviews.

You Might Want to Use Industry-Specific Job Boards

The major job sites make it their business to aggregate all the opportunities listed on most job boards, including the ones on industry-specific job boards. However, it never hurts to supplement your search by including an industry-specific board in your list of tools. These sites often have content beyond just jobs that can help you network or find additional training.

Use a Human Recruiter (If You Can)

Recruiters let you skip the robots and get directly in front of a human. Sometimes they even know about job openings before they are posted. Recruiters can also help you fine-tune your resume, coach you on what to say during an interview, and are out there pitching you to employers. All of this comes at no charge—there is no reason not to accept a recruiter's help.

Monster and Indeed Are Both Good Supplemental Job Search Tools

The two titans of the old-school job industry are still around. Both of them are aggregators that let you search all the jobs in one place, and both of them have enough data to build powerful modern search algorithms. It makes sense if you have the time to set up email alerts from one of these two sites as a supplement to ZipRecruiter and LinkedIn.

Chapter 7: Apply to These Jobs

You do not want to be "black holed" where you apply but never hear anything back from prospective employers. Here are some guidelines to make sure you get a response and some additional rules for what makes a good job to apply to:

Apply to Jobs Within The First Two Days They Are Posted

Applying to a job within two days of the job being posted **more than doubles your odds of getting hired**. The longer you wait to apply, the lower the odds your application will be considered. Employers view only 50% of applicants who come in after the first seven days.

Don't Self-Disqualify

The employers writing job postings are creating a wish list—not an accurate description of who they will hire. Give yourself permission to **apply for any job where you meet 40% or more of the requirements**.

Apply to Jobs That EXACTLY Match the Most Recent Job Title on Your Resume

Any time your current (or last) job title matches the title in the posting, you have higher odds of getting put in front of a human. This is why your resume should list the most common description of the role you filled. No one is going to report you to the resume police for making your work history easier to understand.

Apply to Jobs Where You Know Someone at the Company

Over half of jobs are filled by a candidate who already knew someone at the company. When you have someone on the inside vouch for you, not only is it more likely that your resume will be seen by the person with the power to set up an interview, but it's coming from someone the company already trusts. Many companies even encourage these types of referrals, paying out bonuses to employees that bring in new hires.

Apply to Jobs Where You Love the Company, Product, or Service

If you're passionate about a company or what they do, go ahead and apply. If you can get in front of a human, your passion and expertise for the product, service, or industry they work in will make you a great interview.

Apply to Jobs That Are Closer to Where You Live

Long commutes breed misery and unhappy employees. Employers know that, which is why **employers like candidates who live closer to the office,** and are wary of applicants who live farther away. This may change for some positions, now that the pandemic has expanded remote work. But it will likely remain true for positions that must be done in-person.

Apply to Jobs with Stated Compensation That Is Higher Than What You Currently Make

The surest way to get a salary bump is to move to a new company. Compensation is a concrete way to compare one job to another and a succinct way to clarify to yourself, and hiring managers, why you are looking to leave a current role. As a result, **target jobs that offer more money than you're currently making.**

Apply to Jobs at Direct Competitors of Your Current Employer

Your industry expertise makes you an ideal candidate to the hiring manager because they know you'll hit the ground running, and your inside knowledge of a competitor means you carry a currency that no other candidate on the market can match.

However, think *hard* before you make this choice. Unless you get the blessing of your current company, this strategy is fraught with not just relationship risk, but actual legal peril. Check your employment agreement with a lawyer to make sure you haven't signed a binding noncompete clause. You'll also want to be extremely careful not to bring any of your prior company's intellectual property to your new job.

Apply to Jobs Where the Employer Has Reviews Online That Pique Your Interest

Read reviews about a potential employer, including details about work culture, diversity, management, and salaries. **Reading reviews can help you identify the right company for *you*,** and will also give you great content for your interview to show that you came prepared.

Should You Send a Cover Letter with Your Application?

Because printed resumes are no longer mailed to a hiring manager, **a cover letter isn't required 99% of the time.** If you find yourself in the rare situation when a human being actually places your resume directly into another human's hands, make sure your letter addresses the reader specifically, remains brief, highlights your personality, and uses the correct formatting.

What If I Want to Change Industries?

Whether you just don't like what you do or you have to change industries because of technological disruption, new careers are well within your reach.

Explore "new-collar" opportunities—jobs that require expertise in only a single skill, software, or technique. Many of these jobs can be had after relatively short training courses. Examples include piloting a drone, photo and video editing, sound production, computer-aided design (CAD), business management software, home inspection, massage therapy, medical device operation, phlebotomy, and many more.

Do NOT Apply to These Jobs

Watch out for phony employers and job scams designed to take advantage of people who are desperate for work. Some warning signs of a scam job are: having to pay to get the job, a requirement to share credit card or bank account information, or the promise of access to otherwise private government jobs.

If anyone offers high pay for little work or extends an offer without even speaking with you, run the other way. **Three particularly dangerous job scams are:**

- Jobs that ask you to receive and send packages (**repackaging scams**).
- Jobs that ask you to receive and transfer funds (**money laundering scams**).
- Call-center jobs that ask you to sell a sham product or service and collect people's financial information (**call center scams**).

Think Twice Before You Apply to These Jobs

A job is supposed to pay you, not the other way around. **There are some risky jobs that you should be careful before accepting.** Two of the most prevalent high-risk jobs are multilevel marketing (MLM) and lease–purchase truck-driving jobs.

- **Multilevel marketing jobs** pitch you the ability to sell a popular and well-known brand of some product on your own time, and promise you that your earnings are only limited by how hard you work. But the catch is that you need to buy a supply of the products first, and that it's much harder to get your friends, family, and strangers to buy products from you than most people think. Even worse, MLM companies encourage you to spend a lot of time recruiting others to become salespeople, which critics argue is really just a pyramid scheme, which is illegal.

- **Lease–owner trucking** companies will pay you to go through a truck-driver training program, but when the program is done, they'll entice you to buy your own truck using their financing. Unfortunately, the costs quickly multiply, and are deducted from your paycheck. It's not uncommon to get negative paychecks for which you owe them money. Lease-owner trucking jobs can be a hard way to make a living driving a truck. Many trucking companies have paid millions to settle class-action lawsuits against them.

Chapter 8: How to Ace a Pre-Screen

A lot of employers will pre-screen you before bringing you in for an interview. This is usually just a verification exercise. This is *not* an interview. It is dead simple to get past this step. Here's how to navigate the phone screen hurdle.

Read Your Email And Answer Your *&#%* Phone

Employers *hate* when they can't get in touch with you. Once you've applied to a job, **check your email regularly and have your phone on you.** Take every call—even if your caller ID marks the call "Unknown." That's all you have to do to give yourself a better shot at success.

This Is NOT the Time to Ask Questions

Pre-screening calls are formulaic exercises in confirming your key skills and work history. Don't caveat your answers or ask questions about their questions. Answer as simply and directly as possible. It's okay to be imprecise. You can offer clarity when they bring you in for an in-person interview.

It's Okay to Be Excited

Enthusiasm during the pre-screening call helps you, and is persuasive to the person on the other end of the conversation, even if all they are doing is checking some boxes. **Smile while you're talking.** The simple act of smiling releases feel-good hormones that help relax your body, and lower your heart rate and blood pressure.

Chapter 9: What to Wear to an Interview

In the first twenty seconds of your interview, your interviewer will reach numerous judgments, which are unlikely to change regardless of how long they speak with you. As a result, first impressions are critically important. What the interviewer sees in the first twenty seconds—your clothes and demeanor—will play a *huge* role in whether you win the job.

Understand the Unconscious Bias Around Apparel

Studies have shown strong bias around apparel. People who wear what is perceived to be "expensive" clothing are judged as more competent. Since what you wear influences your interviewer's first impression, buying a new outfit is an investment that can pay off big. **You don't need to spend a lot of money on clothes for your interview.** There are a number of fast fashion retail stores now that make looking stylish affordable. **Just remember to iron your new clothes before you wear them!**

Picking Your Interview Outfit

Not all jobs have the same dress code. There is no one-style-fits-all outfit that works for every interview. **Pick clothes that *you* think make you look good.** When you feel good, it changes your posture and boosts your confidence.

How You Know Your Interview Outfit Is Right

The only important rule for an interview outfit is that you're wearing something that makes your brain think you look good! When you feel confident, you'll naturally "power pose" in which your shoulders set back, your chest puffs out, and your arms relax. The right interview outfit literally changes how you carry yourself and interviewers will notice. **Keep shopping until you find an outfit that makes you want to kick ass!**

Perfume and Cologne are a Definite No

Make sure the defining thing your interviewer remembers about you is *not* how you smell. **Go to every interview scentless.** No perfume, cologne, aftershave, baby powder, body lotion, or hair spray.

Let's Talk About Sweat

When you sweat, others view you as less confident, less competent, and less trustworthy. To keep yourself cool and dry, you can wear antiperspirant, wear a cotton undershirt, use sweat pads, carry a kerchief or scarf, hold a cup of ice water, refrain from alcohol the night before your interview, and don't drink caffeine on the day of your meeting.

Chapter 10: How to Ace a Job Interview

A full 93% of job seekers feel nervous about interviewing. Here's how to stay calm and make a standout impression.

Don't Die in the First 20 Seconds

You can't win the job in the first 20 seconds, but amazingly, you can lose it. There are four things you need to do as soon as you meet your interviewer:

1. **Give a REAL smile**, which involves a contraction of the muscles around both your mouth, *and* your eyes.
2. **Make strong eye contact** immediately. This heightens their perception of your confidence, elevates your perceived social status, increases their belief in what you have to say, and triggers multiple parts of the brain involved in empathy, which means your interviewer will be primed to connect with you. (After that first conscious use of eye contact, go back to your normal eye contact pattern. Too much eye contact in conversation signals you are "selling," which is associated with dishonesty.)
3. **Offer a firm handshake**, which signals confidence and extraversion.
4. **Say the name of the interviewer**, and add "nice to meet you." Saying their name is viewed as a compliment because it was important enough for you to remember, and also increases feelings of familiarity so that both of you relax.

How to Crush the Next 29 Minutes and 40 Seconds of the Interview

After the first 20 seconds comes the trap question: "**Tell me about your-self ...**" No one *ever* wants you to really answer this question. Instead, I am going to tell you *exactly* what to say.

The Magical First Sentence

This magical first sentence is your powerhouse opening to kick off what will be a great interview: "[INSERT INTERVIEWER NAME]—(*one-second pause*)—**I'm so excited to be here because [fill in the blank with some-thing specific about the business.]**" You know the magical first sentence worked if your interviewer immediately starts talking.

Hit the Ball Back Every Time

Great interviews are when the two parties spend an *equal* amount of time talking. They are trying to figure out what it would be like to work with you and will learn more from how well you listen, what questions you ask, and how you process new information, than they will from listening to you talk about yourself.

Your goal is to start conversations. Not deliver monologues. **Make a game of ending every answer you give with a question.** In essence, after everything you say—I want you to "hit the ball back."

Standing Out

An interview is a contest with only one winner. You aren't just trying to prove you can do the job, you're trying to prove you can do the job better than all the other candidates you're competing against. There is one thing that the best candidates do to cement their status as top pick: **create a mem-orable moment,** which is when the interviewer feels like they've taught you something, made you change your mind, or took an idea you brought in with you and made it better.

How to Create a Memorable Moment

Interviewers are more likely to remember you if they feel like *they* did well in the interview. How do you make your interviewer feel great? When your interviewer asks you a question, take a full two seconds before responding.

Show them you're thinking about what they said and that you're a thoughtful listener. Everyone loves a great listener.

"I Have a Story to Tell You . . ."

Want to be *really* memorable? Get your points across by telling stories. **Facts are 20 times more likely to be remembered if they're delivered as part of a story.** Interviewers are asking you questions in the hopes of starting a conversation. Nothing captures attention and makes a person want to share back more than a good story. And your greatest tool for doing so is this sentence: "I have a story to tell you . . ." **Rehearse at least two stories so you have them in your back pocket when you go into the interview.**

Be Ready for These Common Interview Questions

After "tell me about yourself," there are two questions that trip up job seekers more than the rest.

- **"Why are you looking to leave your current job?"** There is no answer you can give to this question that meaningfully increases your chances of getting hired, but there is one answer that is *definitely* wrong: **don't say *anything* negative about the last boss you worked for, or worse, the company itself.** No matter how valid your complaint, denigrating your current or previous employer, will always reflect poorly on you.
- **"How much are you looking to get paid?"** The answer to this question is *not* whatever your last job paid plus a slight bump. The answer to this question is what the market will bear! **Do your research online and know the market rate for the role.**

There are a dozen other common questions it pays to be prepared for:

- "Why do you want to work at this company?"
- "Why do you want this job?"
- "What are your greatest strengths and weaknesses?"
- "Tell me about a work conflict and how you dealt with it?"
- "Why are you changing careers?"
- "What's your management style?"
- "What do you do when you're not at work?"

- "Where do you see yourself in five years?"
- "What would your 30/60/90 day plan be?"
- "How many bathroom stalls are there in a New York City skyscraper?"

"Do You Have Any Questions?" Yes, You Do!

You should always have questions at the end. Asking questions (and the quality of the questions you ask) is one more way to *show* versus *tell* the interviewer what it will be like to work with you. You want to show that you're thoughtful about the business, care about culture, and importantly, that you are interested.

How to Be Awesome in a Video Interview

In a postpandemic world, video interviewing is certain to be a fixture in the future of work. With video interviewing, instead of twenty seconds to make a first impression, you get just one second. But the good news is that you have 100% control and can stage every detail of what your interviewer sees when they first virtually meet you. Here's a list of things to do to make sure you own every part of your first impression.

- **Overgroom yourself**, which means selecting solid color outfits, using hair styling products, shaving your face or brushing your beard (for men), considering a ponytail (for women or long-haired men), using makeup to cover up blemishes or bags under the eyes, cleaning your glasses, wearing pants, tidying your eyebrows, and making sure you use the "touch up my appearance" setting on Zoom.
- **Pick a spot with good light**. It's best to sit facing a window to get natural light, but sitting outside in the sun or using your own inexpensive lighting setup are also good options.
- **Place your camera at eye level**, using books or anything else to prop the camera up higher.
- **Check your background** to make sure that everything in the camera's eye leaves a good impression and doesn't look cluttered or messy.
- **Sit up straight**. Posture matters, and an upright spine conveys professionalism and attentiveness.
- **Smile when you join the call**, so that the first thing people see when your video appears is your smile.

- **Show interviewers you're into it** by starting with the "magic sentence." Let them see you using a pen and paper to take notes.
- **Embrace the unexpected** by realizing that something is likely to go wrong and remembering that, when it does, handling things well will end up reflecting positively on you.

Chapter 11: How to Follow Up After the Interview

Only 43% of candidates send their interviewer a thank-you note after an interview, which makes it easy for people who want to stand out. There are three techniques to writing a follow-up thank-you message, but all of them follow the overriding golden rule: **talk about the interviewer— not yourself!**

Increase Your Enthusiasm . . . Because You Met Them

There is no better way to compliment interviewers than to **say meeting them increased your interest in the role.** Confirm what they suspected— that they were great in the interview!

Show You Listened to Them

Repeat something you learned or a key takeaway you had from speaking with them. Limit yourself to one or two examples, and share how their words affected you.

Highlight Their Best Moment

Revisit their best moment from the interview by either rehashing the best question they asked, revisiting a moment they changed your mind, or describing a moment they taught you something.

Part Three: Go Get That Job!

Chapter 12: You Must Negotiate

Your Brain Is Stupid

In a 2018 survey of more than 50,000 job seekers on ZipRecruiter, 64% reported accepting the first offer they received.[1] For most people, negotiating is painful. It's not your fault. It's how your brain is wired. To your muddled brain, negotiating might cause the employer to rescind the offer. Let me reassure you that your brain is *stupid*. Employers *do not* rescind job offers because you ask for more.

You Get What You Negotiate

Pay in MOST salaried jobs is set by negotiation. There are some jobs where negotiating is not possible, but for the vast majority of jobs employers **expect you** to negotiate.

Negotiation Is Expected, and Priced into the First Offer

According to ZipRecruiter's 2018 job seeker survey, about one-third of all job candidates attempt to negotiate their job offers. Because they don't know which ones it will be, **employers discount their first offers by between 5% and 15% to *all* candidates**. Before negotiating with an employer, spend five minutes researching and equipping yourself with the data you need to get a good idea of your value in the marketplace.

They Can't Guess What You Want

Before you enter a negotiation, **make sure you've thought about the other things you might want in addition to the job and salary**. Think about things like a flexible work schedule, more vacation time, your moving expenses covered, your job title, a good parking spot, or even bringing your dog to work. If you can't get everything you want in a negotiation, be prepared to trade something less important to you for something more important.

Don't Negotiate Against Yourself

A lot of job seekers fail to use these three fundamental tactics before accepting a job.

First, **apply to more jobs**, which ideally will get you multiple offers, which in turn is more likely to lead to a higher initial offer.

Second, **anchor higher** by suggesting a salary at the high end of the range. You can easily find out what the market will bear here: www.ziprecruiter.com/Salaries. Don't be afraid to throw out the first number in a negotiation.

Finally, **never accept the first offer.** A single ten-minute negotiation is likely worth more than $15,000 to you over the next four years.

Chapter 13: Negotiating Your Job Offer—A Step-by-Step Guide

Step 1: Celebrate with the employer as soon as you get the offer. Doing so will make them think of you as part of the team, triggering anxiety about losing you.

Step 2: Make a smooth counteroffer with one of these approaches.

- The **"name your price"** approach, in which you say, "If you can do (x), we have a deal."
- The **"one small problem"** approach, in which you say that you love the company, but you have "just one small problem you need to solve" before accepting the offer. The problem is yours and yours alone, but by sharing it you give them the opportunity to offer a solution.
- The **"multiple offers"** approach, in which you go out and get more than one company interested in hiring you. The four most powerful words in any negotiation are, "I have another offer." If you're someone that doesn't like negotiating, getting a second offer is the key to inducing employers to bring up their offer without you saying a word.

Step 3: Say nothing until they do. This is easy. After you've made a counteroffer to the employer, don't say another word. Just remain silent, no matter how awkward it gets.

Step 4: Accept the offer correctly. When the employer says, "we have a deal" make sure you ask for the offer in writing. Also, don't sell past the close, which means not rehashing any negotiation points or saying anything other than how excited you are about the agreement. And shift immediately to saying "we" over "me." Use inclusive language to indicate you're on the team now and accelerate your integration.

Chapter 14: How to Quit Your Current Job the Right Way

Leaving a job in the right way is crucial to protecting yourself, your reputation, and your relationships. By doing everything you can to soften the blow, you're making an investment in your future.

Don't Quit Your Job Until You Have an Offer Letter in Writing

No matter how confident you are that you're starting a new job, **do not talk to anyone about it at your current job until you have an offer letter in writing**. Of course it's unlikely that something will go wrong before you get the offer in writing, but it's not impossible, so play it safe.

Always Notify Your Direct Manager First—Don't Skip Levels

The first person you should notify about quitting your job is your direct manager. When you do it, make sure you give them at least two weeks, notice, explain why you accepted the new job, and ask for input on how to best communicate that you're leaving to the rest of the team. For extra credit, you should also offer to assist in hiring a replacement for yourself, and write down a summary of your responsibilities and suggestions on who best to offload each responsibility to. You should also offer to train someone internally in all your responsibilities before you leave.

No Touchdown Dances

Your actions on the way out are how the company and members of your team will remember you. Do whatever you can to cushion the blow of you leaving, which includes not doing any overly exuberant celebrations in front of your current colleagues about either your new job or the things you won't miss about the current one. If you want to celebrate, celebrate them by telling them how much you both enjoyed and learned from working with them.

What to Do If They Counter

There's a chance that your employer might make you a rich offer to entice you to stay. Before you jump at the money, make sure to think hard about why you were leaving in the first place. If you're going to accept a counter, make sure they address more than just the cash you're dissatisfied with, and **make your asks big**. If you accept the counter, **tell the other company immediately**.

Also, don't be surprised if you remain unhappy after accepting a counteroffer, because **50% of employees who accept counteroffers still end up leaving within a year**. Don't beat yourself up if you find yourself back on the market shortly after getting everything you thought you wanted.

Chapter 15: Congratulations on the New Job! Let Me Know How It Went!

If you've followed all my advice, then it's only a matter of time before you're ready for this last step: Celebrate!

You've worked hard to find your new job, so make sure to take some time and enjoy your accomplishment.

Nothing gets me and the ZipRecruiter team more fired up than helping people find work, so please reach out and tell me your job search story at www.ziprecruiter.com/gethirednow.

Notes

Chapter 1: Accept the Truth About Bias

1. Anthony C. Little, Benedict C. Jones, and Lisa M. DeBruine, "Facial Attractiveness: Evolutionary Based Research," *Philosophical Transactions of the Royal Society B: Biological Sciences* 366, no. 1571 (2011): 1638–1659.
2. Janine Willis and Alexander Todorov, "First Impressions: Making Up Your Mind after a 100-ms Exposure to a Face," *Psychological Science* 17, no. 7 (2006): 592–598.
3. Frank Dobbin and Alexandra Kalev, "Why Diversity Programs Fail," *Harvard Business Review* 94, no. 7 (2016): 14.

Chapter 2: Write a Resume That Works

1. Kerri Anne Renzulli, "75% of Resumes Are Never Read by a Human—Here's How to Make Sure Your Resume Beats the Bots," CNBC, February 28, 2019, www.cnbc.com/2019/02/28/resume-how-yours-can-beat-the-applicant-tracking-system.html.
2. "Eye-Tracking Study Ladders 2018," The Ladders, 2018, www.theladders.com/static/images/basicSite/pdfs/TheLadders-EyeTracking-StudyC2.pdf.
3. "Wonderlic Employer Soft Skills Survey Spring 2016," Wonderlic, 2016, https://wonderlic.com/wp-content/uploads/2017/06/Wonderlic_National_Employer_Report_Survey.pdf.
4. "Cancer Statistics," National Cancer Institute, September 25, 2020. www.cancer.gov/about-cancer/understanding/statistics.

Chapter 3: Polish Your Online Brand

1. CareerBuilder, "More than Half of Employers Have Found Content on Social Media That Caused Them NOT to Hire a Candidate, according to Recent CareerBuilder Survey," Press release, August 19, 2018.
2. Accounttemps, "Check Your References," Robert Half, March 11, 2019.

Chapter 4: Network to Build Relationships

1. Danielle Elmers, "The Job-Search Statistics All Job Seekers Should Know," TopResume, March 4, 2020, www.topresume.com/career-advice/7-top-job-search-statistics.
2. Lou Adler, "New Survey Reveals 85% of All Jobs Are Filled Via Networking," LinkedIn, February 28, 2016, www.linkedin.com/pulse/new-survey-reveals-85-all-jobs-filled-via-networking-lou-adler/?src=aff-lilpar.
3. Thomas A. DiPrete, Andrew Gelman, Tyler McCormick, Julien Teitler, and Tian Zheng, "Segregation in Social Networks Based on Acquaintanceship and Trust," *American Journal of Sociology* 116, no. 4 (2011): 1234–1283.
4. Mark S. Granovetter, "The Strength of Weak Ties," *American Journal of Sociology* 78, no. 6 (1973): 1360–1380.
5. Erin Griffith, "How One Founder Used Instagram Likes to Earn $500K in New Business," *Fortune*, February 14, 2014, https://fortune.com/2014/02/14/how-one-founder-used-instagram-likes-to-earn-500k-in-new-business/.
6. Penenberg, A. (2012, August 04). Social Networking Affects Brains Like Falling in Love. Retrieved January 08, 2021, from https://www.fastcompany.com/1659062/social-networking-affects-brains-falling-love
7. Namsu Park, Kerk F. Kee, and Sebastián Valenzuela, "Being Immersed in Social Networking Environment: Facebook Groups, Uses and Gratifications, and Social Outcomes," *CyberPsychology & Behavior* 12, no. 6 (2009): 729–733.
8. R. Matthew Montoya, Robert S. Horton, and Jeffrey Kirchner, "Is Actual Similarity Necessary for Attraction? A Meta-Analysis of Actual and Perceived Similarity," *Journal of Social and Personal Relationships* 25, no. 6 (December 2008): 889–922.
9. Tobias Langner, Jennifer Schmidt, and Alexander Fischer, "Is It Really Love? A Comparative Investigation of the Emotional Nature of Brand and Interpersonal Love," *Psychology & Marketing* 32, no. 6 (2015): 624–634.
10. L. A. Rivera, "Hiring as Cultural Matching: The Case of Elite Professional Service Firms," *American Sociological Review* 77, no. 6 (2012): 999–1022.
11. Ovul Sezer, Francesca Gino, and Michael I. Norton, "Humblebragging: A Distinct—and Ineffective—Self-Presentation Strategy," Harvard Business School Marketing Unit Working Paper 15-080 (2017).

Chapter 5: Use Job Sites That Have These Features

1. ZipRecruiter, Inc. internal data.
2. ZipRecruiter, Inc. internal data, January 2016 to December 2020.

3. Sreshtha Das, "How Does a Resume Parser Work? What's the Role of AI?" AI in Recruitment, July 1, 2020, https://skillate.com/blog/resume-parser/.
4. Chandlee Bryan, "The Early Bird Gets the Job," *StartWire*, June 2, 2011, www.startwire.com/blog/6107618938.
5. ZipRecruiter, Inc. internal data, July 2020 to December 2020.
6. ZipRecruiter, Inc. internal data, January 2020 to December 2020.

Chapter 6: Tools You *Have* to Use in Your Search

1. iOS App Store data/Google Play Store data, December 2019.
2. Jobvite. "2020 Recruiter Nation Survey," October 2020, www.jobvite.com/wp-content/uploads/2020/10/Jobvite-RecruiterNation-Report-Final.pdf.
3. Catherine Fisher, "5 Steps to Improve Your LinkedIn Profile in Minutes," LinkedIn official blog, August 3, 2016, https://blog.linkedin.com/2016/08/03/5-steps-to-improve-your-linkedin-profile-in-minutes-.

Chapter 7: Apply to These Jobs

1. Chandlee Bryan, "The Early Bird Gets the Job," *StartWire*, June 2, 2011, www.startwire.com/blog/6107618938.
2. Kushal Chakrabarti, "The Science of The Job Search, Part III: 61% of 'Entry-Level' Jobs Require 3+ Years of Experience," TalentWorks, 2018.
3. Danielle Elmers, "The Job-Search Statistics All Job Seekers Should Know," TopResume, March 4, 2020, www.topresume.com/career-advice/7-top-job-search-statistics.
4. Umeå University, "Long-Distance Commuters Get Divorced More Often, Swedish Study Finds," *ScienceDaily*, May 2011, www.sciencedaily.com/releases/2011/05/110525085920.htm.
5. Dan Buettner, *Thrive: Finding Happiness the Blue Zones Way* (National Geographic Books, 2011).
6. David C. Phillips. "Do Low-Wage Employers Discriminate against Applicants with Long Commutes? Evidence from a Correspondence Experiment," *Journal of Human Resources* 55, no. 3 (2020): 864–901.
7. PRNewswire, "Nearly One-Quarter of Workers Have Left a Job Due to a Bad Commute, According to Robert Half Survey," news release, September 24, 2018.
8. Jim Harter, "Employee Engagement on the Rise in the U.S.," Gallup, November 11, 2020, https://news.gallup.com/poll/241649/employee-engagement-rise.aspx.

9. Edison Research, "The Infinite Dial 2020," Edison Researchblog, March 19, 2020, www.edisonresearch.com/the-infinite-dial-2020/.

10. "Nielsen At Podcast Movement 2020: Opportunities in a Skyrocketing Industry," Nielsen, November 17, 2020, www.nielsen.com/us/en/news-center/2020/nielsen-at-podcast-movement-2020-opportunities-in-a-skyrocketing-industry/.

11. National Conference of State Legislatures, "The National Occupational Licensing Database," March 2020, https://www.ncsl.org/research/labor-and-employment/occupational-licensing-statute-database.aspx.

12. "Freelance Forward 2020," Upwork, September 2020, www.upwork.com/documents/freelance-forward-2020.

13. "Complete List of Direct Sales and MLM Companies Worldwide," LaConte Consulting, LLC, 2020, https://laconteconsulting.com/mlm-list/.

14. Marguerite DeLiema, Doug Shadel, Amy Nofziger, and Karla Pak, "AARP Study of Multilevel Marketing: Profiling Participants and Their Experiences in Direct Sales," AARP, August 2018, www.aarp.org/content/dam/aarp/aarp_foundation/2018/pdf/AARP%20Foundation%20MLM%20Research%20Study%20Report%2010.8.18.pdf.

15. Jon M. Taylor, "The Case (for and) against Multi-Level Marketing," Federal Trade Commission, 1999, https://www.ftc.gov/sites/default/files/documents/public_comments/trade-regulation-rule-disclosure-requirements-and-prohibitions-concerning-business-opportunities-ftc.r511993-00008%C2%A0/00008-57281.pdf.

16. "19 Amazing MLM Statistics You Should Read in 2020," Jobs in Marketing, February 19, 2020, https://jobsinmarketing.io/blog/mlm-statistics/.

17. "Big Rigged," NPR, August 14, 2020, www.npr.org/transcripts/901110994.

Chapter 8: How To Ace a Pre-Screen

1. Seventy-Five Percent of Workers Who Applied to Jobs Through Various Venues in the Last Year Didn't Hear Back From Employers, CareerBuilder Survey Finds. (n.d.). Retrieved January 08, 2021, from http://press.careerbuilder.com/2013-02-20-Seventy-Five-Percent-of-Workers-Who-Applied-to-Jobs-Through-Various-Venues-in-the-Last-Year-Didnt-Hear-Back-From-Employers-CareerBuilder-Survey-Finds

2. Ronald E. Riggio "There's Magic in Your Smile," *Psychology Today*, June 25, 2012.

3. Amy Drahota, Alan Costall, and Vasudevi Reddy, "The Vocal Communication of Different Kinds of Smile," *Speech Communication* 50, no. 4 (2008): 278–287.

Chapter 9: What to Wear to an Interview

1. Tricia Prickett, Neha Gada-Jain, and Frank J. Bernieri, "The Importance of First Impressions in a Job Interview," presentation at the annual meeting of the Midwestern Psychological Association, Chicago, IL, 2000.
2. Dong Won Oh, Eldar Shafir, and Alexander Todorov, "Economic Status Cues from Clothes Affect Perceived Competence from Faces," *Nature Human Behaviour* 4, no. 3 (2020): 287–293.
3. Adam Hajo and Adam D. Galinsky, "Enclothed Cognition," *Journal of Experimental Social Psychology* 48, no. 4 (2012): 918–925.
4. Joel D. Mainland, Andreas Keller, Yun R. Li, Ting Zhou, Casey Trimmer, Lindsey L. Snyder, Andrew H. Moberly et al., "The Missense of Smell: Functional Variability in the Human Odorant Receptor Repertoire," *Nature Neuroscience* 17, no. 1 (2014): 114.
5. "Scientists Uncover New Connection between Smell and Memory," *Science Daily*, July 23, 2018, www.sciencedaily.com/releases/2018/07/180723155726.htm.
6. Alexandra D. Sifferlin, "Don't Let Them Smell You Sweat: You'll Seem Untrustworthy," October 9, 2013, https://healthland.time.com/2013/10/09/dont-let-them-smell-you-sweat-youll-seem-untrustworthy/.
7. "Tips for Reducing or Stopping Sweating," *Medical News Today*, updated September 25, 2019, www.medicalnewstoday.com/articles/326441#summary.

Chapter 10: How to Ace a Job Interview

1. JDP, "2020 Interview Survey," accessed December 1, 2020, www.jdp.com/blog/how-to-prepare-for-interviews-2020/.
2. Leeanne Harker and Dacher Keltner, "Expressions of Positive Emotion in Women's College Yearbook Pictures and Their Relationship to Personality and Life Outcomes Across Adulthood," *Journal of Personality and Social Psychology* 80, no. 1 (2001): 112.
3. Richard A. Tessler and Lisa Sushelsky. "Effects of Eye Contact and Social Status on the Perception of a Job Applicant in an Employment Interviewing Situation," *Journal of Vocational Behavior* 13, no. 3 (1978): 338–347.
4. Takahiko Koike, Motofumi Sumiya, Eri Nakagawa, Shuntaro Okazaki, and Norihiro Sadato, "What Makes Eye Contact Special? Neural Substrates of On-Line Mutual Eye-Gaze: A Hyperscanning fMRI Study," *Eneuro* 6, no. 1 (2019).

5. Frances S. Chen, Julia A. Minson, Maren Schöne, and Markus Heinrichs, "In the Eye of the Beholder: Eye Contact Increases Resistance to Persuasion," *Psychological Science* 24, no. 11 (2013): 2254–2261.

6. Joyce E. A. Russell, "Career Coach: The Power of Using a Name," *Washington Post*, January 12, 2014, www.washingtonpost.com/business/capitalbusiness/career-coach-the-power-of-using-a-name/2014/01/10/8ca03da0-787e-11e3-8963-b4b654bcc9b2_story.html.

7. Diana I. Tamir and Jason P. Mitchell, "Disclosing Information about the Self Is Intrinsically Rewarding," *Proceedings of the National Academy of Sciences* 109, no. 21 (2012): 8038–8043.

8. "New CareerBuilder Study Unveils Surprising Must Knows for Job Seekers and Companies Looking to Hire," Press Room | Careerbuilder, June 1, 2016, http://press.careerbuilder.com/2016-05-31-New-CareerBuilder-Study-Unveils-Surprising-Must-Knows-for-Job-Seekers-and-Companies-Looking-to-Hire.

9. Bart Turczynski, "2020 HR Statistics: Job Search, Hiring, Recruiting & Interviews," Zety, updated October 13, 2020, https://zety.com/blog/hr-statistics#job-search-statistics.

10. "Hard Facts About Soft Skills," 2016, Wonderlic, http://docs.wixstatic.com/ugd/cceaf9_ec9ed750296142f18efdd49f4930f6d3.pdf.

11. Michael F. Dahlstrom, "Using Narratives and Storytelling to Communicate Science with Nonexpert Audiences," *Proceedings of the National Academy of Sciences* 111, Supplement 4 (2014): 13614–13620.

12. Boris, V. (2019, February 04). What Makes Storytelling So Effective For Learning? Retrieved January 08, 2021, from https://www.harvardbusiness.org/what-makes-storytelling-so-effective-for-learning/

13. Janine Willis and Alexander Todorov. "First Impressions: Making Up Your Mind after a 100-ms Exposure to a Face," *Psychological Science* 17, no. 7 (2006): 592–598.

Chapter 11: How to Follow Up After the Interview

1. "These 5 Simple Mistakes Could Be Costing You the Job," CareerBuilder, June 10, 2019, www.careerbuilder.com/advice/these-5-simple-mistakes-could-be-costing-you-the-job.

Chapter 12: You Must Negotiate

1. "Employee Tenure in 2020," Bureau of Labor Statistics, September 22, 2020, www.bls.gov/news.release/pdf/tenure.pdf.

2. Amy Stewart, "PayScale Survey Reveals the Compensation Best Practices of 2020," PayScale, March 11, 2020, www.payscale.com/compensation-today/2020/03/payscale-survey-reveals-the-compensation-best-practices-of-2020.

Chapter 13: Negotiating Your Job Offer—A Step-by-Step Guide

1. Marc T. P. Adam, Gillian Ku, and Ewa Lux, "Auction Fever: The Unrecognized Effects of Incidental Arousal," *Journal of Experimental Social Psychology* 80 (2019): 52–58.

Chapter 14: How to Quit Your Current Job the Right Way

1. "Why People Quit their Jobs," *Harvard Business Review*, September 2016, https://hbr.org/2016/09/why-people-quit-their-jobs.

Appendix: Before You Start the Search

1. "The Employment Situation—April 2020," U.S. Bureau of Labor Statistics, May 8, 2020, www.bls.gov/news.release/archives/empsit_05082020.pdf.
2. Julia Pollak, "A Golden Age for Veteran Job Seekers," ZipRecruiter blog, November 2019, www.ziprecruiter.com/blog/golden-age-for-veteran-job-seekers/.

Summary

1. Julia Pollak, "The ZipRecruiter 2018 Annual Job Seeker Survey," ZipRecruiter blog, 2018, www.ziprecruiter.com/blog/ziprecruiter-2018-annual-job-seeker-survey/.

About the Author

1. iOS App Store data/Google Play Store data, December 2019

Acknowledgments

I'd like to say thank you to our ZipRecruiter economist Julia Pollak for helping put this book together, Benny Spiewak and Marc Fienberg for research, Ward Poulos for design, and Matt Spangler for the comic illustrations. And another thank you to the hundreds of ZipRecruiter employees around the world who have worked with me over the past 10 years to connect millions of people to their next great opportunity.

About the Author

Ian Siegel is the CEO and cofounder of ZipRecruiter, an AI-powered jobs marketplace and the top-rated job search app in the United States.[1] Ian has dedicated the past 10 years of his life to developing better ways for people to find jobs and employers to recruit talent. Over that time he has spoken with thousands of job seekers and hiring managers, built a team of data scientists to pull insights from the billions of user interactions in the ZipRecruiter marketplace, and closely followed the third-party research on who gets hired, how, and why. Ian has been interviewed on the topics of how to get a job, the job market, and the future of work for multiple news networks including Fox Business, CNBC, and Bloomberg, as well as being featured in *the Wall Street Journal, USA Today*, and *the New York Times*.

Index